A DOG'S GIFT

A DOG'S GIFT

THE INSPIRATIONAL STORY OF VETERANS AND CHILDREN HEALED BY MAN'S BEST FRIEND

BOB DRURY

Principal photography by Joan Brady

RODALE.

© 2015 by Bob Drury

Rodale books may be purchased for business or promotional use or for special sales. For information, please write to: Special Markets Department, Rodale Inc., 733 Third Avenue, New York, NY 10017

Printed in the United States of America

Rodale Inc. makes every effort to use acid-free ♾, recycled paper ♻.

Unless otherwise noted, all photographs © Joan Brady

Book design by TheEuclidShop

Library of Congress Cataloging-in-Publication Data is on file with the publisher.

ISBN 978–1–62336–101–3 hardcover

Distributed to the trade by Macmillan

2   4   6   8   10   9   7   5   3   1   hardcover

We inspire and enable people to improve their lives and the world around them.
rodalebooks.com

For ADDIE, the cornerstone upon
which paws4people was built

Contents

Introduction

An Accidental Destiny

TERRY HENRY CRIES EASILY. OH, AS A FORMER NAVY MAN, AIR FORCE counterintelligence operative, and State Department security specialist, I've seen him act the tough guy on many occasions. But I've also witnessed Terry's tears flow at the memory of the disabled children and traumatized veterans with whom he has placed Assistance Dogs, and his eyes often glisten when he talks about the grace of his daughter, Kyria, or where his own force of fate has led him. I find this admirable.

I do not cry easily. I guess I fancy myself the same sort of tough guy. Streetwise crime reporter. Hard-bitten war correspondent. Wore those labels like a suit of armor, until I met Terry and began chronicling the wonder of the work he and Kyria do. So I suppose the fact that I have cried with Terry on more than one occasion is a testament not only to the lives he has changed but also to the path he has chosen. Either that or I am just a sucker for watching a sick and lonely child's unbridled joy at getting a dog.

Terry is the executive director and, in his words, "chief groomer, kennel cleaner, and dog bowl washer" of the nonprofit organization paws4people and its several offshoots, including paws4vets, paws4prisons, and paws4reading. A lean and pensive fifty-nine-year-old whose round and smooth baby face and inquisitive blue eyes are offset by his gruff public persona, Terry started paws4people fourteen years ago with Kyria out of his Virginia home after accompanying his daughter and her pet Golden Retriever, Riley, on a visit to a nursing home.* It was serendipity. The frail and often ill seniors reacted to the dog with an energy that shocked the facility's staff, not only playing and chattering with Riley but also interacting with each other as never before.

Terry watched the animal's emotional effect on these elderly shut-ins, and something just clicked. In what he now refers to as a blindingly idiotic idea, he quit his second career as a telecommunications engineer and threw himself into the cause of healing others through the power of dogs. He has not stopped since, despite financial, personal, and emotional setbacks. Moreover, paws4people has attracted hundreds of industrious and loyal volunteers and is on the verge of huge institutional changes. Yet the organization still feels like the pop-and-daughter outfit that manages to survive on a shoestring budget of private donations.

Over the past twelve years, Terry and Kyria—now twenty-seven and teaching college courses in Assistance Dog Training—have placed their dogs free of charge with more than four hundred children and veterans in need. Considering that each puppy they raise costs close to $35,000 to house, feed, and train before the dog can even "get to work," the financial and emotional burden has sometimes seemed unmanageable, if not futile.

Terry often drives long distances—hundreds of miles—picking up his dogs from training centers or delivering them to clients. And though he is loath to wear his religion on his sleeve for friends

---

* All of paws4people's Assistance Dogs' names are officially registered in capital letters. For purposes of reader clarity and function, in this book, dogs such as RILEY will be rendered as Riley.

and strangers alike, he admits to listening to spiritual and inspirational books on tape during these journeys. He once told me that he believes absolutely in the philosophy of life espoused by Rhonda Byrne in *The Secret* —that your uplifting thoughts can be made manifest in real life if you believe strongly enough—and has taken to heart the preachings of evangelicals such as the charismatic Texas pastor Joel Osteen.

"When we were at our nadir, when the times were so hard that we didn't know where we'd get the money for the next bag of dog food, it was our faith that got us through," Terry said one night as we strolled the lawn of paws4people's rustic headquarters in Wilmington, North Carolina. A new moon had risen in the October sky, and its hard, bright light danced through the branches of the pine trees swaying above us.

"During this one particular down period, I remembered something I'd listened to from one of Joel Osteen's sermons . . . "

And here Terry paused, as if looking for just the right words. I waited as the moon's lovely shadows played across the ground. Finally he said, "It was about just concentrating on the positive, about no matter how many times you get knocked down, keep getting back up. About how God sees your resolve and determination. And when you do everything you can do, that's when God will step in and do what you can't do. And I reminded myself what a blessing it is that I can be doing this work.

"Think about it," he continued. "I've had the pleasure and privilege of seeing these disabled kids we help regain a little more normalcy in their lives. Of seeing these broken veterans we help to get back on their feet. What on earth do I have to complain about?"

At this I was surprised to see a tear form in his eye and roll down his cheek, and it struck me that Terry, like Shakespeare's

Hamlet, believes "there is a divinity that shapes our ends." It was also at that moment that I decided to write this book.

—————————

As Terry and Kyria visited more and more nursing homes as the years passed, Kyria badgered her reluctant father into acquiring more dogs. In a short time their kennel grew to five Golden Retrievers, and the life-affirming reactions of the seniors to the visiting dogs continued to astound and impress Terry. By the time Kyria entered her teens, she had also convinced her dad to turn his attention to special ed classrooms. So while Kyria concentrated on helping teenagers with special needs in her own high school—kids born with physical or mental disorders, or suffering from debilitating illnesses and syndromes—Terry began traveling to local grade schools with the dogs to work with even younger children who were similarly afflicted.

Through trial and error and by reading as much of the literature as they could get their hands on (Kyria would even spend a summer at acclaimed trainer Bonnie Bergin's University of Canine Studies in northern California), Terry determined that Golden Retrievers and Labradors, or some mutt-mix thereof, made the ideal Assistance Dog breeds. "Just the right combination of temperament, compassion, loyalty, and—to be honest—dumbness" is how he explains it.

"It's not that we have anything against, say, German Shepherds. They make wonderful Seeing Eye Dogs. But what makes them so good at that job is the fierce, fierce loyalty to their blind owners. They will protect their owners to the death. Well, that won't work when your owner is a former combat vet having a public breakdown and the German Shepherd won't let the EMTs near him. Perhaps there is one in a thousand German Shepherds out there who would be ideal for our program. But we can't afford to bring in the other 999 to find out."

The phrase *Assistance Dog* is an umbrella term for all dogs trained to mitigate disabilities in humans—psychological Service Dogs, Seeing Eye Dogs, Therapy Dogs, and mobility Service Dogs, for instance, all fall under the category of Assistance Dogs—and Terry suspects there are other members of the hundreds of currently recognized canine breeds whose social skills would allow them to fare well as Assistance Dogs were it not for their scary public image. He specifically mentions Rottweilers and Great Danes. But, he acknowledges, some dogs just do not have the disposition for any type of service. He cites Irish Setters, for example, as far too high strung (as is obvious to anyone who has ever known one) and Poodles as too intelligent.

"Poodles will learn quickly how to turn a light switch on and off," he says, "or fetch medicine from closed cabinets and refrigerators. But after a few weeks, they become bored with the repetitiveness of the jobs."

So because of these things, paws4people has settled primarily on Retrievers and Labs. Terry and Kyria either breed or receive as donations newborn puppies from accredited and selected breeders who have shown themselves willing to forgo any revenue—although, as Terry is a sucker for sob stories, the occasional rescue mutt has been known to sneak into the mix.

The majority of service-dog organizations limit themselves to one of two tasks: either breeding or training. Paws4people is one of the few outfits that do both. After a litter is born or acquired, the puppies live and socialize together for eight weeks under Terry's and Kyria's watchful eyes before beginning their "schooling." There is a purpose to this: Pups remain rather helpless through

this infant stage—a fact rare among most animals, both domesticated and wild—and tend to form an attachment to whatever species they first come into contact with. In the case of paws4people
dogs, that would be humans. After all, for an animal that is one
day going to work as an Assistance Dog, it makes sense that its
first encounters should be with a person. Another benefit of this
"leisure time" is that it allows a pup to shed any fearful or even
predatory instinct it may feel toward man or woman.

When the eight weeks have passed, the dogs are enrolled in
an eighteen- to twenty-four-month "basic training" that includes,
of all things, an early stint behind bars. Through an agreement
with the West Virginia federal and state prison authorities, the
dogs are trained by both male and female inmates to respond to
nearly one hundred commands that gradually escalate from the
rudimentary "sit," "heel," and "come" into the more sophisticated
and instrumental "brace," "alert," and "light switch." The
paws4prisons program is part of a rehabilitation process sanc-
tioned by the Bureau of Prisons, and Terry and Kyria have hired
several of the inmate trainers upon their release.

As for the dogs, Terry jokes that "once sprung," they undergo
a more intense Service Dog training regimen, including a rigorous
Public Access program with professional trainers and later with
potential clients. This instills in the animals discipline and a work
ethic that separate them from your average pet.

The length of training time varies, depending upon a dog's
temperament and ultimate placement. Though many of the tasks
overlap, Assistance Dogs can basically be separated into two categories: Indirect Service Dogs—that is, Educational Assistance
Dogs that work in special ed classrooms and Social Therapy
Dogs that visit hospitals, children's libraries, nursing homes, and
even some residential psychiatric treatment facilities—and Direct

Service Dogs, which are placed with clients in need of mobility Service Dogs, psychological Service Dogs, or a combination of both.

When paws4people first branched out into special needs classrooms, Terry watched with an awe bordering on disbelief as the dogs performed what he called miracles with the kids, much as they had in the nursing homes. One young boy born with a portion of his brain missing so took to one dog that he progressed from refusing to speak to learning to count out loud and recite the alphabet. And a little girl confined to a wheelchair with cerebral palsy was among the many who began to walk with a dog's help. It struck Terry that if the presence of one of their animals could open up new vistas for these children with disabilities, why could it not do the same for the estimated half million American servicemen and women returning from foreign battlefields with emotional and psychological wounds?

Thus, paws4vets was born. And that's where I came in.

I never planned on being a reporter or writer, much less a foreign correspondent where, you know, the hazards of the profession include nasty, crazy people shooting at you. Still, I suppose it beats working.

As the oldest child of a hard-charging and hard-drinking son of Ireland's County Mayo, two of my major life-shaping influences were my father's belt being applied liberally to my hindquarters and the Dominican nuns and Benedictine priests and brothers who educated me, respectively, through grammar school and high school. I was the oldest of four, and I have joked to my two younger sisters and "baby" brother that they should thank me that Dad exorcised all his bad parenting by the time they came along.

Ours was the kind of home, for instance, where if I walked in from high school with a welt on my face that coincidentally matched the shape of the Dean of Discipline Father O'Leary's fist, my parents demanded to know what I had done to provoke him. This is why I have never, ever laid a hand on my own son.

That said, I did inherit from my mom a love of reading; comic books and *The Hardy Boys* were favorites early on, and by my early teens I had devoured all of Sir Arthur Conan Doyle's Sherlock Holmes mysteries. When it came time for college—the Jesuits this time, sparking later-in-life ruminations about my gluttony for punishment—against my father's business-minded wishes, I majored in English. Naturally, this allowed me to consume and reconsume *The Hobbit* and *The Lord of the Rings* trilogy like one of those bridge painters you hear about who finally finishes at one end only to begin again on the other side.

Upon graduation, I had no idea what I might want to do other than move to Cape Cod and chase girls. It was while working as a commercial fisherman off the Cape that I stumbled into a newspaper job covering town council meetings and Cape Cod League basketball games—twenty dollars a story bought a lot of beer in those days. When I set out for New York City, I was lucky enough to find work covering sports for one major newspaper, the police beat for another, and overseas news for a third.

Thus, it happens that I have written extensively about our military since 9/11, both in Iraq and Afghanistan as well as here at home. My reporting included myriad visits to military treatment centers, such as the National Naval Medical Center and the Walter Reed Army Medical Center. And it was at these facilities that I first saw how medical professionals were struggling to understand and cope with the long-term ramifications of psychological and emotional symptoms caused by post-traumatic stress disorder

(PTSD) and traumatic brain injury (TBI). From the earliest days of our wars, these hospitals had been using visiting Therapy Dogs to, in essence, raise the spirits of wounded troops. But the notion of employing long-term psychological Service Dogs that would remain with a veteran for life seemed to go against the military's martial DNA. Although attitudes have since changed dramatically, the majority of combat vets were initially loath to admit they needed mental help. For the most part, their superiors agreed.

This is why it took Terry and Kyria years to convince the Department of Defense that their dog therapy was indeed a worthwhile experiment. But finally, in early 2010, they received the go-ahead to begin a pilot program to train psychological Service Dogs for the Wounded Warrior Battalion at Fort Stewart, a sprawling US Army base on the outskirts of Savannah, Georgia. This is where Terry and I first met. Believe me, he initially struck me less as a latter-day Florence Nightingale and more as a human drill bit stuck on full bore. In fact, as I observed him in action during those first few days, I thought he was the meanest man on earth.

It began one sweltering afternoon when we gathered in a modular trailer on a far corner of Fort Stewart that served as the paws4vets headquarters. Seated in a semicircle around Terry were seven wounded warriors—six males and a female—who were being instructed to serve as dog trainers. The group was the first class of volunteer trainers on the base, and their Assistance Dogs lay at their feet. Most of these soldiers had been scarred by bullets, mortar shells, or blasts from improvised explosive devices, modern warfare's ubiquitous IEDs. Each also suffered from some form of PTSD or TBI—two names as synonymous with misfortune as Smith and Wesson—what Terry calls the invisible disabilities.

According to a recent study by the Rand Corporation, about

19 percent of US troops deployed to Iraq and Afghanistan may have sustained physical or psychological brain disorders from explosive devices or exposure to traumatic events. That would be about 380,000 soldiers, sailors, airmen, and marines. The Rand study also noted that different soldiers react to stress in different ways.

Some of the soldiers in the trailer had returned from overseas deployments and refused to leave their darkened barracks rooms. Others were spooked by the sights and sounds of a fireworks display or a shadowed highway overpass or even a brightly lit and crowded supermarket. A few had lashed out at fellow GIs and superior officers; one in particular, a violent man with teeth like a crazy fence, had become quite well known around Fort Stewart as a source of trouble in the form of constant fistfights. And the lone woman, a shy and pretty member of the National Guard with the rank of specialist, had been abandoned by her unit in the Iraqi desert and left to fend for herself. She was now wracked by severe depression and anxiety that led to panic attacks.

All had one thing in common: War had changed them, beaten them. And life back home had proven more baffling and tormenting than combat itself—until they met their dogs. Most of these soldiers hoped to take one of Terry's dogs home with them upon their medical discharge. But they understood that this would depend not only on their progress as dog trainers but also on their ability to instruct the next generation of servicemen and servicewomen who would take their places.

As I watched the give-and-take between Terry and the group, I was struck—as I always am around soldiers—by how young these warriors were. Each had once been an ordinary American kid, hailing from towns with names like Poverty Slant, Harmony, or Gunpowder Rapids. Now they were all connected by what Abraham Lincoln called "the mystic chords of memory." If it is true, as the famed Prussian military theorist Carl von Clausewitz said, that war is the best teacher of war, these shattered young professionals had known it as few others had, and the roaring fury of combat had seemed to squeeze their minds down to the size of clenched fists.

Terry and Kyria believe that dogs have the uncanny ability to transfer the psychological pain and suffering of humans into themselves—"to absorb it like a sponge," as Terry puts it, and then shed it like winter fur. There is a cost to this, he adds. The process physically exhausts the animal. And I was surprised to find the commander of Fort Stewart's Wounded Warrior Battalion, a veteran lieutenant colonel, agreeing with this metaphysical proposition. As he told me one day over breakfast, "It's almost like there are electric currents coursing through the leashes, connecting the minds of the soldiers with the minds of their dogs."

On my first day at the military base, the paws4vets group had spent the morning with Terry in a fenced-in compound they had constructed themselves, practicing a drill that teaches the dogs to ignore each other while concentrating completely on their handlers—one of the hardest tasks for an Assistance Dog to learn. As I watched these wary soldiers brighten and step out of their shell-shocked cocoons with the help of the bounding canines, a grizzled forty-four-year-old staff sergeant named Vernon Ward sidled up next to me and cocked his chin toward the dog compound. He was hard as a sandbag, with hair as thick and white as an arctic fox's.

"When I first enlisted, the word *malingerer* was in common usage," he said in a drawl gravelly enough to walk on. "But we don't say that anymore. Things were different then. We didn't know as much about the human mind as we do now."

Staff Sergeant Ward had twenty-seven years of service on his résumé, including combat deployments to Panama, Somalia, and Iraq. Now he was the NCOIC, or noncommissioned officer in charge, of the base's paws4vets pilot program, and I could hear the pride in his voice when he added, "With this program, it's just a fact, sir, not a theory, how those dogs have reduced the level of anxiety in my wounded warriors."

A few hours later, in that sweltering modular trailer, the levels of anxiety were definitely back on the uptick. For it was obvious that Terry was not happy. I squirmed uncomfortably as he scolded one enlisted man for allowing his Labrador to remain so "growly" during the drills and admonished another for giving his Golden Retriever a treat despite the fact that she had left his side to sniff another dog's butt. He even threatened the female specialist with expulsion from the program for not being commanding enough with her voice.

"Since the last time I was here, what has your dog taught you and what have you taught it?" he demanded of a hulking staff sergeant named Paul Tully who was ruffling the scruff of the only rescue dog, some kind of terrier mix, that had been adopted into the program. The dog's name was Tazie, and after an American soldier rescued her as a puppy from a feral pack of dogs in Afghanistan, paws4vets arranged for her to be brought to the States. Tazie and Staff Sergeant Tully, whose neck had been broken in Iraq, had been together since the pilot program's inception. But when the sergeant failed to answer Terry's question quickly enough, he pounced.

"People, I got to be honest. I'm more concerned about my dogs than I am with you."

His voice resounded through the cramped room like the downbeat of an ax, and the group was reduced to staring down at their scuffed combat boots. I said nothing.

But the most disturbing aspect of Terry's tough love was his treatment of the army veteran Jeff Mitchell, the only member of the Fort Stewart program who had already been medically discharged from the service. Jeff had served two deployments in Iraq, beginning in 2003 as a specialist with the 2nd Howitzer Battery of the 3rd Armored Cavalry Regiment. His tours had left him with such a devastating case of PTSD that many thought there was no hope for his recovery. He had witnessed friends wounded and killed in the most horrible circumstances—limbs and lives lost to roadside IEDs hidden in deflated soccer balls or dead animals. In one raw letter to his parents, Carol and Doug, he recorded the experiences of his first firefight.

"The first explosion shook everything, and the shock waves caused ripples in the ground as if you threw a stone into a pond," he wrote. "I saw a civilian running from the blast; he was thrown 200 feet into the air. [There were] earth-rattling explosions, huge balls of fire and mushroom clouds, and red, white, and orange pieces of burning metal blown into the sky. I heard the whistling of incoming rounds and saw hunks of metal flying through the air along with tracer rounds and still more explosions. That same night . . . grenades were thrown; six of my buddies were hit. I wasn't afraid at the time because everything happened so fast and I reacted automatically because of my training. We are lucky to be alive."

More of the same followed during Jeff's second deployment to Tal Afar, a dangerous city north of Baghdad—more combat, more IEDs, more deaths of friends. In 2006, Jeff returned home riven with flashbacks and hallucinations, which he tried to block out with alcohol. But his condition came to a head one night on leave when he struck his girlfriend, hard, as she woke him from a nightmare. Back on base, he refused to leave his barracks, and he was medically discharged.

By the time Jeff returned to his childhood home in Atlanta, doctors from the Veterans Health Administration had prescribed him such a menu of mood-altering drugs that he could barely remember how many pills he was taking each day. He entered his old bedroom, dimmed the lights, locked the door, and found a liquor store that delivered. He became—in military medical slang—a "cave dweller." And in that cave he remained until the night his mother, Carol, knocked on his door and asked if he might be interested in meeting a psychological Service Dog.

Desperate, Carol had reached out to Terry and Kyria after reading an article about paws4vets, and they had agreed to enroll Jeff in the Fort Stewart program. He had been a part of it for six months now, teamed with the Assistance Dog Caroline, a two-year-old Golden Retriever. Speaking to Jeff was not an easy task; he was so close to catatonically uncomfortable with strangers that his eyes could not meet my gaze. And his tics—crinkling his nose, constantly adjusting his glasses, tapping his feet to a pneumatic beat—were on full display. Yet he managed to open up enough to tell me how the connection he had developed with his Assistance Dog was gradually helping him to adjust to civilian life.

"In these last six months, I've done things and gone places for the first time in four or five years," he said. "To the grocery store. To get my hair cut. Out to dinner with my parents. These were things that I'd stopped doing. I'd stopped participating in society around me. I just withdrew and stayed locked in my room for years."

As he spoke, he nervously ran his fingers through Caroline's coat, as if she was his living, breathing security blanket. "I've been pretty removed from any feelings or emotions for such a long time," he continued. "And sometimes I'm still overwhelmed thinking about the future. But as we go forward, Caroline and me, over months or years, I know I'll get better."

I got the sense that after his life was upended by the horrors of war, Jeff was hanging on to his Service Dog as a lifeline to the civilian world he had long ago left behind. And this is why I was so taken aback when Terry announced to the Fort Stewart group that afternoon that if Jeff did not begin to show more progress, if Terry did not begin to see more of a connection between Jeff and the dog, he was strongly considering taking Caroline away from him.

Then, turning to Jeff, Terry's eyes narrowed as he said, "You're not putting in the effort, not really trying, and you're hurting my dog, which is my first concern. You use Caroline when you feel you need her, when you feel the old tears coming on. But then when you don't feel you need her . . . "

And here Terry paused, apparently measuring his next words. "I can see it in the dog, Jeff. You're not as connected to her as she wants to be to you. It's too much of a one way street with you. Going forward with Caroline is not your decision. You will never be able to make that decision. We have the final say-so on whether Caroline stays with you. It all depends on whether you show me, not tell me, how much you want this."

Stunned silence followed. And then it got worse.

Following the session, Terry, myself, S.Sgt. Ward, and the six other wounded warriors all piled into trucks to accompany Jeff and his dog to Fort Stewart's Post Exchange, or PX, where he was to take a Public Access progress exam. An army base's PX is similar to a huge military-themed Walmart or Costco, and one month earlier, the last time Jeff had been here, Terry had asked him to walk through the store with the dog. Jeff had not been able to handle the crowds, the bright lights and colors, the white noise from scores of conversations, ringing cash registers, and public address announcements. He collapsed in front of the sushi bar not ten feet from the PX's front door and rolled into the fetal position on the floor feeling, he'd told me earlier, as if he were stranded in a literal minefield. It had taken Terry and the others forty-five minutes to help him up and out.

Now, this afternoon, Jeff was being offered a second chance, perhaps a last chance. As he took his first tentative steps, our entire group held its collective breath. When we exhaled, word began to spread in low voices.

"He made it past the sushi."

"He's up to the cereal aisle."

"Now he's at the laundry soap."

Jeff would intermittently pause to kneel beside Caroline, composing himself while he gently caressed her scruff with both hands. The Service Dog—that metaphorical sponge absorbing Jeff's fear and anxiety—huddled in close to him and licked his face. Some shoppers gave this odd couple a cursory glance, but most breezed past them oblivious. Jeff walked up and down every aisle in the PX, and as he neared the checkout line, our small circle felt our relief turn to genuine joy for his courage—well, almost everyone in our small circle.

Terry had been trailing Jeff and Caroline at some distance, maybe twenty-five feet, and he stood off to the side with a dour look as Jeff exited the building and immediately seemed to deflate, the strength draining from his body as if he had sprung holes.

When Jeff sat down on the curb, his head between his knees, breathing hard, Terry barked, "Pay attention to Caroline. Give her a treat. Yes, you did it. But you couldn't have without her. Thank her. Show her some love."

Jeff hopped up, his hands still shaking, and cuddled Caroline. He fed her several treats. As the others mobbed him with congratulations, I stared at Terry in disbelief. Once, at Walter Reed Army Medical Center, I had witnessed an army captain who had lost both of his legs to an IED blast in Afghanistan viciously berate a young corporal with a prosthesis on one leg for not running hard enough around the track in the center's gym.

The captain had lost one of his legs above the knee and one below the knee—he was an AK and a BK in the military medical parlance—while the jogging corporal was "just" a BK.

"I've seen two AKs run faster than you, corporal," the captain bellowed. "You expect people to feel sorry for you, you expect the United States government to pay for your care and feeding, when you are not even trying worth a goddamn. I'll put on my legs and come out there right now and run you into the ground!"

The corporal picked up his pace. The captain winked at me.

Now, at Fort Stewart, I tried to convince myself that this was what Terry was doing to Jeff. Yet it still didn't feel right.

Later that night, in a quiet moment at our hotel, I confronted Terry about his verbal lacerations of these poor soldiers, Jeff in particular. In truth, I felt like punching him in the nose. I expected him to be defensive. Instead, he sighed and rested a hand on my shoulder. For the first time since I'd met him, his face creased into a soft, warm smile.

"I know I looked like a jerk out there today," he said. "But trust me, I want Jeff to succeed; I want them all to succeed. Because I know exactly what they're going through. And if this is the only way to make them better . . . "

Terry's voice trailed off as we locked eyes. He took in a breath.

"You know how I know that?" he said. "Because I've suffered from PTSD for over 20 years. I was a drug addict, addicted to prescription pain killers. There were times when I felt like killing myself. And Kyria, the dogs, paws4people, they were the lifeline that brought me back. And though I can sometimes hide it well, it's always with me. Sometimes I still feel exactly like they do in that dark, scary place. Like being trapped in a well that you think you'll never be able to climb out of.

"Jeff Mitchell has to *want* to climb out of that dark and scary well. You don't know Jeff that well yet, but I do. Nobody can lift him out. But what I can do is throw him a lifeline. And if a part of that lifeline is taking his dog away, letting him know that I'm serious about Jeff making Jeff better, then that's what I'll do.

"This is what I preach," Terry said finally, "you have to be involved in something bigger than yourself if you want to beat PTSD. Because PTSD just drains you, just opens the spigot and sucks you dry if you let it."

I was stunned. I had read the man completely wrong. Terry understood better than most that Jeff Mitchell, that all of the soldiers in the group, felt as if they were stranded in a lonely place, with mundane plans instead of hopes. It dawned on me that if music is the space between the notes, then Terry's long silences, and even his reprimands, were the culmination of his faith—faith in these wounded warriors, faith in the healing process, and his faith in a higher power.

"The only time I will ever give up on Jeff, give up on any of them, is when they give up on themselves," he said. "If Jeff does give up, give up on his dog and his parents and me, I'm through with him. There are too many others out there who want to help themselves. I've got to devote my energy to them. Unfortunately, I know this from experience."

Then Terry winked. Winked! Just like the captain at Walter Reed.

"But I don't think that's going to happen."

Not long after that conversation, Terry indeed took Caroline away from Jeff. Jeff and his parents were devastated. But that is not the end of Jeff Mitchell's story. Despite Jeff's protestations, Terry's own vicious bout with PTSD had given him a judicious sense of what not to believe in others who also suffer from the syndrome. He knew Jeff was slacking. But Terry had a plan for Jeff. A plan that included, of all things, Tazie the Afghan rescue mutt.

Once I heard that, I decided then and there to spend the next year immersing myself in all things paws4people, in meeting and talking with the organization's volunteers and teachers and clients and trainers. I wanted to discover—if, indeed, there was anything to discover—if there could possibly be such a powerful connection between dogs and humans that could result in, well, miracles. And over the following months that I spent observing and traveling with Terry and Kyria and some of the paws4people volunteers, Jeff's and Tazie's plan was not the only one that I would witness play out.

Moreover, during that time, Terry Henry and I would together climb an emotional mountain of our own. The result of that ascent is this book. It is a story about love and faith. A story about battered combat veterans and profoundly disabled children. A story about dogs and the astounding healing powers they have on bruised and bent human beings.

Unless you are a dog lover, or at least a dog owner, you may not believe that premise. I confess to my own doubts as I began this journey. No more. The polymath W. G. Sebald once wrote, "Men and animals regard each other across a gulf of mutual incomprehension."

With all respect to Sebald's genius, Terry Henry and I beg to differ.

Chapter One

Birth

" Bob! It's time. Get down here."

There is an urgency to Terry's voice that I've never heard before. I roll out of bed, check my watch, and take the stairs two at a time. It is nearing midnight as I reach the whelping room, sliding across the floor like a cartoon character in my stocking feet. A rumpled Terry is on his knees in the penned-in nursery, cradling Claire's furry head in his arms. He is wearing his trademark uniform of khaki cargo pants, a black T-shirt, and a dark fleece, the clothes creased six ways from Sunday as a result of sleeping on an inflatable air mattress on the floor next to the laboring Golden Retriever.

"Come on, baby," he whispers in a tone as soft as church music. "That's right. Everything's okay. We've done this before."

The five-year-old Claire is about to give birth to her third litter of puppies. Although some female dogs can deliver up to the age of seven or eight, Terry and Kyria have decided that this will be Claire's last. Throughout this pregnancy, she has been acting "a little off," in Terry's words. "More jumpy; not eating right."

Claire is not technically due for another three days. But this afternoon—day sixty of a dog's typical sixty-three-day gestation period—her temperature dropped from 101 to 98 degrees, and earlier this evening she had ignored a bowl of milk, shredded lamb, and rice that Terry had nudged under her nose. Her lack of appetite worried him, and he sensed that she would drop the pups prematurely.

Now Terry runs a hand through his salt-and-pepper brush cut as thick as otter fur and glances up at me with a weary smile. "Contractions started," he says. "Kyria's on her way."

In an adjacent room, a temporary kennel, five curious dogs—three Goldens and two Labs—jostle against the door gate for a better view. Terry and Kyria have only relocated from northern Virginia to their new North Carolina headquarters in the past week—I am their first guest—and parts of the two-story building still resemble a construction site, while the scent of disinfectant fills the entire facility. I follow Terry's gaze as he juts his chin toward a table in the corner piled high with folded quilts and towels, the clean laundry stacked beside a box holding balls of yarn in various colors.

"If you could hand me a blanket," he says, "and maybe start cutting that yarn into pieces of, oh, twelve inches or so."

Yarn? The only birth I have ever been present for was my son Liam-Antoine's, fifteen years ago, and I am certain I would recall if there was a need for yarn. We were in a French maternity hospital north of Paris—Liam-Antoine's mother is French—and I vividly remember the array of gleaming instruments on a table to the side of her birthing bed. The forceps. The medical scissors to snip the umbilical cord. Even the pan in which the placenta would eventually be placed. But no yarn. Terry seems to read my thoughts.

"When the puppies arrive, we mark their birth order and time. Claire's x-ray showed eight, and things are going to get a little hectic around here. We weigh them and tie a different-colored piece of yarn around each of their necks to remember who's who for the records. I'll need your help keeping track."

He turns back to Claire and gently urges her to push while he adjusts the two heat lamps on either side of the whelping pen. The joke around paws4people is that Terry loves dogs more than he likes people. Actually, from what I've seen so far, it's really not a joke at all. It is among dogs that I have seen him most relaxed. But Claire is even more special to Terry. A few years back, his beloved Golden Retriever Addie, his own personal psychological Service Dog who helped him cope with his PTSD, died suddenly. Terry was devastated and went into a blue funk. Finally, at Kyria's insistent urgings, he began seeking Addie's successor, and after several starts and stops with potential dogs, he met Claire, with whom he developed a strong bond. Claire was in fact still being trained and groomed as Terry's dog when he noticed the calming effect the dog had on a navy veteran named April Cook.

April had approached paws4vets seeking help three years earlier, and Terry immediately sensed the emotional connection between her and Claire. When Claire nuzzled and cuddled with her, April visibly relaxed, to the point where she almost seemed a different person. Her old self, maybe. Terry could only guess.

What he did know was that April had enlisted soon after 9/11 and survived four deployments to Iraq as part of a helicopter medical evacuation and combat search-and-rescue unit. During those tours, she had helped triage scores of wounded and dying American soldiers. April had always thought of herself as an outgoing and vivacious person, curious as to the ways, whys, and wherefores of the world. It was one of the reasons, along with a strong sense of patriotism, that she had joined the navy after high school. Yet following each deployment into combat zones— downrange, as American servicemen and women refer to it—she suspected that her personality was slowly changing.

"It's hard to explain," she would later tell me. "Like something in my soul was eroding and making me more and more skittish and jumpy and just kinda nuts. I would bawl like a baby at the tiniest things. Losing my hairbrush. A mouse in my tent. I found I wanted to talk to my crew members less and less. I didn't want to hear their stories. I didn't want to know them too well in case they got killed."

One day, arriving by chopper to tend to the survivors of a firefight outside of Baghdad, her medical crew was ambushed by insurgents. Her helicopter's crew chief pushed her out of the way to safety just as a mortar shell exploded nearby. The crew chief was killed instantly. If not for his actions, it would have been April. This incident was the culmination of a long and debilitating two years. During her earlier deployments, she had been sexually assaulted on multiple occasions by a higher-ranking sailor from her unit. When she reported this to his superior officer, she was threatened with a dishonorable discharge. Those traumas seemed to come to a head after the ambush. She served out her remaining time, received an honorable discharge, and returned home with a severe case of survivor's guilt.

It was difficult for Terry to part with Claire, but in April he recognized the dog's true soul mate.

"Maybe there were other dogs that might have pulled April out of her downward spiral," Terry told me. "But I didn't want to take the chance to wait around and find out."

So last year he placed April's well-being over his own and presented her with Claire. He had only been reunited with Claire last week, when April drove her from her home in Fayetteville and dropped her off so she could give birth at the Wilmington center. Since separating from Claire, April had called the center several times each day to check in on her. What kept April functioning emotionally as she attended therapy classes and lived on her military pension was the knowledge that as soon as Claire's pups were finished suckling, she would return to Fayetteville. On a few occasions, April had even asked Terry or Kyria to put the phone to Claire's ear so she could tell her she loved her.

Terry could relate to the emotional connection; since placing Claire with April, he had "taken up" (as he puts it) with another beautiful Service Dog, eight-year-old Chaeney, one of the Goldens now in the kennel in the next room. Chaeney had been the feistiest puppy in the second litter paws4people had ever bred, and Terry jokes that he wasn't sure what to do with this "worthless, untrainable" dog until one day, on a whim, he decided to take Chaeney along to an elementary school's special needs classroom that he and Addie were visiting.

The formerly "worthless" Chaeney blossomed with the children, and he was soon certified as an Educational Assistance Dog with a particular knack for assisting special needs kids prone to violent outbursts. Terry also discovered that when he was with Chaeney, the dog had a soothing influence on his own "black moods." So with Claire gone, Terry turned to Chaeney to be his personal Service Dog, and now he never travels anywhere without him at his side. Yet as much as Terry loves Chaeney, I can see that he still misses his old companion. It is obvious from the way that he now gently massages Claire's distended belly.

"Her water broke about a half hour ago," he says. "She's been really pushing for twenty or thirty minutes."

I find scissors and start snipping yarn while Terry, still stroking Claire, begins to tell me his story.

Terry Henry grew up hopscotching across America's heartland. His father, Jim, a troubleshooting engineer for General Electric, was transferred often, and Terry attended schools in Kentucky, Illinois, and Indiana. It was the Henry home outside of Fort Wayne, Indiana, that he seems to recall with the most fondness—the vast corn fields just across the street that bled into dense woods crisscrossed by creeks. It was in those trees and streams that Terry and the neighborhood kids spent hours constructing forts and building dams. A boy's nirvana.

Terry was the oldest of two; his mother, Pat, who taught in and later ran nursery schools, would give birth to his sister, Joan, two years later. He was a smart and curious child with good grades, and by the time he reached high school, his interests were myriad, including (in no particular order) girls, sports, the military, and dogs. The first three came naturally, his fascination with soldiers increasing with every television episode of *Combat* or *The Desert Rats* and spiking whenever a movie such as *The Longest Day* arrived at the local theater. The fourth was thrust on him. When he was five years old, his mother took in a Collie from her army-bound cousin, and the pet's care and feeding fell on Terry. It was one way, Jim Henry figured, to teach his son about responsibility. It also had another effect.

"That's probably when I fell in love with dogs," Terry recalled.

Except for school, the two went everywhere together; he even brought her to the sandlot and hitched her leash under the stands when he played baseball. When the Collie died of old age, a German Shepherd puppy replaced her in the Henry household, and despite Terry's busy high school agenda, he always made time for her, too. As with the Collie before her, Terry just liked having a dog around, like a good friend.

Meanwhile, Terry had blossomed into a strong athlete who

lettered in football and baseball, but in his senior year his burgeoning career was cut short when he shattered his left arm and shoulder running into an outfield wall. Several surgeries followed, and doctors eventually inserted plates into his shoulder to hold it together. The knowledge that he would never play ball again hurt, but his disappointment was mitigated when the ROTC (Reserve Officers' Training Corps) offered him a full scholarship to pursue an engineering degree at Vanderbilt University, Nashville's venerable "Harvard of the South."

During his first semester at Vanderbilt, Terry secretly adopted another German Shepherd puppy despite the school's prohibition against pets in the dorms. "I had to hide it, sneaking it in and out the window for walks at night and early in the morning," he said while surreptitiously eyeballing the lengths of yarn I laid out on the table.

"I thought I was getting away with something until the end of my freshman year, when this guy comes up to me and says, 'I've enjoyed watching you raise your German Shepherd.' Then he identified himself as the dean of students."

This encounter proved fortuitous. In Terry's sophomore year, he was living off-campus with his pet when one night he and the dog stepped in to prevent some local tough guys from accosting several female students at a mixer. The encounter allowed him to convince the dean of students to form a campus security program, where he got his first taste of what he thought might become a career. Meanwhile, he had also enlisted in the university's naval ROTC program, and he spent his summers training at various military bases throughout the Far East, including a session at the navy's vaunted Philippines Jungle Survival School.

It was there that a bacterial infection attacked his pericardium, the fibrous sac that surrounds the heart. Terry was flown back to the States and underwent a rare and risky operation to remove his pericardium; he endured yet more surgeries when it was discovered that the bones broken in the old baseball injury had failed to knit properly.

Despite these physical setbacks, Terry refused to give up on his ROTC commitment, even going so far in his sophomore year as to enroll in a private flight school to earn his pilot's license. It was his aspiration to fly navy fighter jets, but this, too, was to become another dream deferred. For after he graduated with his engineering degree in 1977, navy physicians informed him that the lingering effects of the pericarditis combined with his bum shoulder precluded him from ever piloting a military aircraft. Sympathetic to Terry's disappointment, his unit commander offered him an out—the Department of Defense was cutting back on active-duty numbers across the board in the wake of the Vietnam War, and the officer suggested that, given his medical history, Terry accept the honorable discharge for which he was eligible. And he did just that.

"They wouldn't let me fly, and I just didn't want to drive ships," he said, dividing his attention between me and Claire and constantly fiddling with the heat lamps. "But ever since the days of watching those war movies, I'd had this longing to be in the military. Plus, they had just paid for my college education, and I felt I owed the government. The other three services were all trimming back, but the air force was still accepting applications. I enlisted and spent the next eight years working in counterintelligence."

At this point, Terry's story becomes murky. He adamantly refuses to talk about his work for air force intelligence or, for that matter, his two years of employment at the State Department that followed through the end of the 1980s. From our many, many conversations, however, I have gleaned that he traveled extensively around the globe. It was on one of those trips, in 1983, where he met and married Debbie, who was also on assignment in Turkey. From my experiences reporting from war zones, I have picked up hints that Terry is, shall we say, not unfamiliar with the echoes of gunfire from his time as an intelligence agent. You get to know a little about a person's background when he is able to describe the difference between a report from a Russian- or Chinese-made AK-47 and an American-manufactured M4 carbine. I have my suspicions about what his job entailed, but I respect his privacy enough to keep them to myself.

Once, when I probed too deeply about the root causes of his PTSD and the decades of therapy he has undergone to relieve the syndrome, his body began to shake, his eyes grew watery, and he pleaded with me to stop.

"I'm not going to talk about that because I can't," he said as tears streamed down his face. "Please don't try to make me. It hurts too deep. You're making me want to jump off a bridge just asking me about it. I won't even address those topics with my therapist. In fact, the therapist I'm seeing now is trying to dig that stuff out of me, and I keep telling him, 'No, No.' I'm ready to leave him because of it."

I have no doubt that Terry is sincere and that somewhere and somehow he went through hell and back. I also suspect that this is the root of his empathy for veterans like Jeff Mitchell and April Cook and why he ultimately founded paws4vets. For it was also during the military chapter of his life that the seeds of his addiction were planted. While training for an overseas assignment in 1985, Terry hurt his back severely enough that he feared that his superiors would cancel the mission, or even reassign him completely, if they found out about the injury. So he contacted a "friendly" doctor who, to ease his agony, prescribed strong dosages of Percocet and Oxycontin—the same addictive opiate that has felled so many professional athletes recovering from injury. Though Terry did not abuse the drugs at first, his back pain never really subsided, and he continued to use the drugs steadily.

He was still spending most of his time abroad when, a year and a half later, Debbie told him she was pregnant. He faced a choice: keep traveling continuously and watch his daughter grow up in brief snatches or find another career. Recalling his own childhood and the safe comfort of family, he left government service. He did not, however, leave behind his need for the prescription drugs. Yet now he found himself ingesting more and more as his PTSD symptoms began to overwhelm him.

With his psychological condition deteriorating and his drug abuse increasing—he would consume up to ten pills a day—Terry fell into a deep funk. He would verbally lash out at anyone, including his wife, over the smallest perceived slights. He moped around the house, refusing to take telephone calls from old friends or coworkers. He stayed up all night staring at the television, although he rarely knew, or cared, what he was watching.

"I bounced from shrink to shrink trying to figure out why I was having all these kinds of problems," he recalled. "I had no idea what PTSD was, and apparently neither did anybody else. This was the early '90s, remember, and I just thought I was screwed up in the head. I didn't even get officially diagnosed until the early 2000s. And then the prescription drugs, well, I've since learned, of course, that that's one of the manifestations of PTSD. Everything collapses around you and you just want to numb your brain. And that's what I was doing. Another word I had never heard of at the time was *agoraphobia*. But I certainly didn't want to go anywhere where there were a lot of people around."

To all outward appearances, Terry and Debbie Henry and their infant daughter lived a normal suburban lifestyle in the

Washington, DC, bedroom community of Round Hill in northern Virginia's Loudoun County. Yet Terry's fear of social interaction was so great that the only employment he could handle was as a short-haul truck driver working through the night. The pay was meager compared to his previous job, but prowling the streets alone on his delivery routes meant he did not have to deal with other people. Moreover, the hours allowed him to spend more time during the day with Kyria, about the only thing that seemed to make him happy.

Little Kyria, Terry felt, was the only person who would not, who could not, "bombard" him with questions about his past and his feelings. Hers was the pure, unadulterated joy of a child with loving parents, and as such, she was really the only person in the world, including his wife and his own parents, with whom he could completely relax, whether that meant watching Disney movies on the couch together or even just playing patty-cake.

Meanwhile, Jim Henry had retired from GE, and he and Pat, both in their midsixties, moved to Loudoun County to be close to their son and his family. This also proved serendipitous, for it was Terry's parents' presence in the neighborhood that ultimately sparked the idea of paws4people. Terry glanced down at Claire and smiled at the memory—about the only thing worth smiling about from that era.

"When Kyria was maybe eight years old, she began taking Riley on visits to my mom and dad. She would notice an almost imperceptible change in them, how happy they were to have Riley around, in particular my dad. At his age he wasn't all that into having a full-time pet, but he loved being with his granddaughter, and if her dog was part of the deal, well, the more the merrier.

"Anyway, Kyria picked up on this mood change and started pestering me. 'If Riley can make Paw-Paw and Mi-Mi happy, why can't I take him to other places to make other people happy?' I could almost see the lightbulb go off over her head. *Let's take Riley to a nursing home."*

Terry exaggerated an eye roll at this. Where would they find the time? He was working dusk to dawn, and the towheaded Kyria was already overcommitted to extracurricular activities. There were dance and equestrian classes. And gymnastics. And cheer-leading. Not to mention schoolwork, where she maintained a straight-A average. And now they were going to start operating a do-gooder community service?

Yet Terry, already feeling guilty about his unstable marriage and his overnight absences, relented and began picking up his daughter after the final school bell and driving her and her dog to local nursing homes.

"Kyria was totally in charge," Terry said, shaking his head at the recollection of his preteen daughter's precocity.

I had to smile at this. In separate conversations, Jim and Pat Henry had also described to me their granddaughter's tendency to be, as Jim called it, "the boss of everyone and everything she came into contact with from the time she could walk and talk."

At Kyria's urging, the Henrys adopted three more Golden Retrievers—Brielle, Oatley, and Addie—and added a fifth, Brinkley, when they bred Riley and Brielle. It was, said Terry, "Kyria who took the dogs to the vet to get their shots, who took them to obedience schools to get their certificates. Everything she did, she put the maximum effort into it. In essence, she started training her first dog at nine, ten years old. That's probably why she's as good at it as she is now. Heck, she's been doing it forever."

As hard as he worked at therapy, Terry was still wracked by his PTSD symptoms, particularly his aversion to meeting and interacting with strangers. He was thus not keen on the idea of having to deal with so many new people in his life, much less dozens of needy senior citizens. But Kyria promised that his only duties would be to ferry her to and from the institutions and keep an eye on her from a distance. In time, however, Kyria began bringing more than one dog on their visits—always with Riley—and Terry would dog-sit for one while Kyria led the other through the facilities.

"I remember standing outside of a room in one of the places as Kyria talked to the residents and thinking, 'That kid's just got a knack for making people open up and feel good while engaging with the dogs.' It came naturally to her, and she'd interact with them on all different levels."

If there was a "grump" among the seniors, Terry said, Kyria would turn that person's mood around to the point where he would start saving lunch scraps for the dogs on the days they visited.

"Kyria would plop down on the floor and feed the dogs from the grump's hand. She'd just ease in right next to him as calm as could be, let him pet the dogs for a bit, and then pop up from her seat and say, 'Okay, we'll see you next time.' This kind of patience from a ten-year-old child? It was unbelievable.

"I tried not to get too involved," Terry continued. "Frankly, I was paying more attention to Kyria than to the dogs and the seniors. But one day I found myself sitting alone with Addie in the lobby when an attendant wheeled a really old woman next to me; she had to be in her nineties. The attendant asked if I minded if she joined us. I said of course not, and Addie kind of snuggled up to her and the woman began petting her. Next thing I know, the woman breaks out in sing-song baby talk, speaking to Addie but calling her by another name. This went on for several minutes, until a nurse walked by, saw what was happening, and stopped in her tracks.

"The old woman stopped talking, and the nurse took her back to her room. I was sitting there wondering if I had done something wrong, when the nurse returned. She still looked sort of stricken. 'That woman hasn't spoken a word in three years,' she told me. Frankly, I didn't know how to respond. And then word spread around the facility, and the seniors began gathering around Addie and me. They were whispering, 'That's the dog. That's the one.' It was like a scene in a science fiction movie."

And here Terry shot another curious glance toward Claire, who continued to breathe heavily on the floor beside him. "That was my first introduction to the power these guys have, the ability they have to hook into people. That was the experience that got me thinking: This is not normal kind of stuff."

By the time Kyria entered Loudoun County High School in 2001, her nursing home visits were the talk of her suburban neighborhood. One day early in the semester, the mother of one of her fellow cheerleaders, an occupational therapist at the high school, asked if Kyria might be interested in bringing her dogs around to her classroom. There were three problematic students in particular that the therapist thought the dogs might be able to reach, two boys diagnosed with "severe and profound" autism and a girl suffering from multiple sclerosis. The boys would not engage in class activities or even leave the room when the rest of the children went outside for recess. And though the girl's physicians had assured her parents and teachers that she was able to walk with assistance, she adamantly refused to leave her wheelchair. Kyria took this as a challenge and, of course, devised a plan.

In my travels with Terry and Kyria, I have noticed that, although it might take a visit or two, most children of all ages take naturally to friendly dogs. And during Kyria's weekly drop-ins to her high school's special ed class, she would allow the autistic boys to pet and brush Riley before placing the dog's leash in the girl's hand. Much to the girl's delight, Riley would then pull her in her wheelchair around the school's outdoor track. Kyria also noticed that the boys would follow their progress from the classroom window. After the first two or three sessions, Kyria set the bar.

"If you want to play with the dog outside today," she told the girl, "you have to get up and walk with her."

To the therapist's astonishment, the girl rose from her wheelchair, took the leash, and, with Kyria and the therapist helping to balance her, shuffled halfway around the track. By the end of the school year, she was completing the entire oval. Meanwhile, the boys had graduated from petting the dogs to throwing balls for them to retrieve. The therapist was ecstatic. *At least they were doing something.* But that was not enough for Kyria, who invented a game wherein the boys were awarded extra time to comb the knots out of the dogs' coats if they would go outside, throw the ball, and actually retrieve it themselves before the dogs reached it. Naturally, Kyria rigged the game, holding back her dogs and allowing the boys to win.

When Terry attended these therapy sessions, he was stunned. To bring a little joy into a lonely senior citizen's life was one thing. To aid an ailing child's healing process—one that medical textbooks cast doubt on—seemed miraculous. The sight of these children responding to Kyria and the dogs also went a long way toward helping Terry pull out of his own PTSD spiral.

"I guess it was because I realized that I was able, through the dogs, to get these kids to do things that other people—their teachers, their therapists, even their parents—hadn't been able to," he recalled. "And looking back on that time from here, the 'wow factor' must have been a big part of it, too. As in, 'Wow, if I can help these little kids, then maybe there's help for me. Maybe I'm not as screwed tight as I think I am.'

"Remember what I told you at Fort Stewart about having to be involved with something bigger than yourself in order to beat PTSD? Well, those first couple of years with those kids, that might have been the first time since I got out of the service that I was doing something selflessly just for the sake of doing it. I think now that this was the beginning of my recovery, that I wouldn't be here right now if it wasn't for those kids."

That may have been the beginning of Terry's recovery, but it was far from the end. Although seeking professional psychological counseling did help Terry to kick his addiction to pain killers, his marriage was under too great a strain. It would last a few more years, but eventually Terry and Debbie separated when Kyria left for college.

"There was no union left," Terry admitted to me. "I'd messed it up so bad, with my total focus on paws4people on top of everything else. She decided that she couldn't stay with that situation, and that the best thing to do was separate."

Meanwhile, newly drug-free, Terry found a job where he could put his engineering skills to work as the director of logistics for a telecommunications company. In a stroke of luck, his new boss was one of the few people at the time familiar with the causes, symptoms, and effects of PTSD. He allowed Terry to set his own hours, so he could arrive after his coworkers had departed for the day and leave before they returned in the morning. He was also given a cubicle far from the rest of the staff, near the building's rear staircase. "I would never use an elevator," Terry said.

"I was better in the sense that I wasn't addicted to drugs anymore," he added. "Better in the sense that at least I understood what was going on with me. I had finally found a therapist familiar with PTSD, who was able to explain to me what was happening."

Here, another grim shake of his head. "But worse from a social-isolation standpoint. Much worse. Just because I understood what was happening doesn't mean it stopped happening. It seemed the more people I met, either through Kyria or on the new job, the less I wanted to deal with them."

Any person living with PTSD—whether a combat veteran or the survivor of, say, a natural disaster or man-made accident, like a car crash—can be overwhelmed by the mundane daily stimuli most of us take for granted. As in Jeff Mitchell's case, a task as simple as walking through a grocery store can put all of one's senses on high alert. The aisles between store shelves, for instance, are referred to by medical experts as the dead space. It is in this dead space where PTSD sufferers see potential threats.

Medical researchers of this phenomenon have discovered that the brain regions that deal with memory and fear, such as the amygdala and the hippocampus, appear to function differently in people affected by PTSD. Brain imaging studies of combat veterans in particular have determined that these men and women are not only more distracted by neutral, or everyday, stimuli, but also by any stimuli that remind them of battlefield trauma—sudden loud noises, a profusion of colors similar to a mortar shell's starburst, an infant's cry. This in turn leaves them in a constant state of hypervigilance.

Fortunately, this condition need not be permanent and can be altered with treatment. In the past, cognitive behavioral therapy was the go-to treatment for PTSD sufferers. But as the once-obscure disorder gained greater public purchase through the experiences of veterans returning from our overseas wars, more recent studies suggest that psychological health providers might need to take a different approach. Enter the psychological Service Dog.

A Service Dog, unlike a therapist, remains by a veteran's side at all times to help that person navigate daily stressors. Since the feedback loop between owner and animal is so constant, the sense of trust built up in PTSD sufferers eases those stressors. While Jeff Mitchell, for instance, may dread entering that dead space between grocery store shelves by himself, he can learn to rely on a dog's instincts that there is no danger there. Still, this rapport takes time, as evidenced by Jeff's breakdown during his first trip through the Fort Stewart PX.

Even in Terry's case, at numerous paws4people public events, I have observed him take a deep breath and force himself to speak at assemblies when it is absolutely necessary. But for the most part, he invariably hangs toward the back of any crowd, a hand running through Chaeney's scruff, huddled into a corner if he can find one, as if trying to blend in with the wallpaper. When I asked why, what exactly was he—is he—afraid of, he opened his mouth as if to speak, but no words emerged for some time.

Finally he said, "It's hard to describe. Sometimes it's like you have the heebie-jeebies, if you know what I mean?"

I knew precisely what he meant.

On my first trip to Afghanistan, not long after 9/11, I was riding with the Northern Alliance—literally riding, mounted atop sturdy little indigenous horses the locals call Marco Polo ponies—when they launched an all-out assault against a troop of Taliban holding a key ridgeline outside of the dusty provincial capital of Khodja Bahauddin, one of the Northern Alliance's last strongholds in the far north of the country near the Tajik border. The firefight lasted all day, and it was a close-run affair until a local warlord and Northern Alliance ally arrived with two tanks and swung the victory.

During the mop-up operations, several Taliban soldiers playing dead sprung up and opened fire. Traveling with our group was a German magazine correspondent and two French radio reporters, a man and a woman. They were sprayed with automatic gunfire and killed on the spot. I was on the other side of the battlefield, but it fell to me to identify the bullet-ridden body of the woman for the local authorities.

Once back stateside in early 2002, I began to be overcome with strange physical symptoms. Nothing in particular would set them off, although it always happened in the late afternoon. My heart would pump as if it were popping out of my chest. My body would tingle all over. In short, the heebie-jeebies.

My initial reflex was to head to the gym, work out as long and as hard as I could, and then drive to my local pub for a couple of beers. This routine staved off the feelings for a while, the combination of physical exercise and alcohol seeming to calm my body. But one day while driving to the gym, the tingling, the heart-pounding became too much. I pointed my Jeep to a local medical clinic operated by a physician friend, walked in, and told him I thought I was having a heart attack.

One year earlier I had undergone a long and thorough heart stress test—which I "passed" with flying colors—and that day my friend the doc was able to have the results of that EKG faxed to his office. When he compared those results with the EKG he administered to me on the spot, he found nothing had changed physically with my heart.

He asked me how long it had been since I had seen the reporters killed and been asked to identify the body. About six months, I told him.

"I'm no PTSD expert," he said, "but from what I understand, that's about when its onset kicks in. Naturally, it wouldn't show up on an EKG."

PTSD? This was so many years ago that people, including me, were not even certain what the initials stood for. It turned out that I was one of the lucky ones. My friend prescribed me a dose of Xanax, which I took for a couple of days until the symptoms faded. They've never really returned, and I've never been formally diagnosed with PTSD—but I still have what remains of that bottle of Xanax tablets somewhere in my freezer, just in case.

I told Terry this story as he sat there cuddling Claire. He looked at me, parted his lips to speak, but then merely nodded as if to say, "Been there, my friend, been there and back."

<hr />

It came as something of a shock to Terry when Kyria approached him the summer before her junior year in high school with yet another proposition. She and the same special ed teacher had submitted a proposal to the local school board asking permission to formally integrate the Henry dogs into an occupational therapy program for students with special needs. The school board had approved the plan, but there was a hitch. Three schools were involved: Loudoun County High School and its two feeder elementary schools. This is when Terry realized he was being set up by his fifteen-year-old daughter.

"I'm beaming with pride, thinking, *Look at my little girl, taking it upon herself to help others less fortunate* and . . . whoa, who the heck's going to take the dogs to those grammar schools while Kyria's going to the high school?"

And here Terry flashed his biggest grin yet. "So I agreed to do the grammar schools for her. Four to five classes each week. That was the hook that got me involved."

He had a lot to study, but Kyria proved an apt instructor. As she had with her dogs, Kyria intuited what her father needed to learn and how and why he needed to learn it. She taught him, for instance, that a strange man's presence could be intimidating to small children, so when he visited the classrooms, it was best to stay low to the ground, on the kids' and dogs' level. This did not help Terry's back pain, but he soon found that the smaller he made himself in a child's presence, the more comfortable the child became.

Kyria also instructed him never to be farther away from the dog than any child. At first he assumed this was for the children's protection. Though around eight hundred thousand Americans require medical treatment for dog bites every year, to this day not one of paws4people's dogs has ever bitten a person, with more than one million official "contacts" between the animals and paws4people clients. But Kyria explained to him that this rule was instead to save the dogs from being unduly poked, prodded, and scratched by either curious kids who knew no better or children who had difficulty controlling their physical impulses.

With Riley, Brielle, and Oatley accompanying Kyria to her high school therapy sessions, Terry began to regard Brinkley and Addie—particularly Addie—as his own. And as he became more comfortable with "his" dogs, he was soon enough developing his own methods for dealing with the kids. He sensed, for example, that children born with Down syndrome, though generally eager to interact with the animals, often still needed him to act as a go-between for them and the dogs.

"Some kids love the sloppy dog kisses and all the drool, but a lot of Down syndrome kids are tactile sensitive," he explained. "So they don't like the dogs slobbering on them. But they love to feed them. So I figured out if I put a child on my knee, he could put the dog treat in my hand, and then Addie would take it from my hand. The kids were in essence giving the treat to Addie, but I was the conduit."

(Treats are essential to the training of Assistance Dogs—or, for that matter, to training animals in general. Most dog trainers operate on the principle of associative learning: Perform a task well, expect a treat as reward. Terry and Kyria landed on individual Froot Loops cereal bits as their go-to treats after experimenting with everything from store-bought dog biscuits to hot dogs and bacon rashers cut into small pieces. And they use Froot Loops to this day. Terry explained with a droll chuckle, "Before Froot Loops, it got a little expensive with the kids popping half of our hot dog and bacon inventory into their own mouths.")

Everything Terry and Kyria trained their dogs to do during these therapy sessions was based on what teachers and parents of special needs children had devised in what are called Individualized Education Programs, or IEPs. These IEP goals, per national educational standards, are established prior to the school year and vary according to each child's needs and abilities. A physically disabled child might be expected over the course of a semester to complete a simple obstacle course laid out on the school grounds in order to prevent her young muscles from atrophying. Or an intellectually challenged child's IEP might call for him to learn the alphabet or to count to twenty.

To adapt to these special needs, Kyria immersed herself in the literature of dog therapy, leaning heavily on studies published by Bonnie Bergin, whose writings on Service Dogs are considered the industry's urtexts. Although Kyria had taken no formal dog training classes at this point, Bergin's example fired some emotion deep within her. Bergin herself had been inspired to start her canine studies school on a trip through Asia, where she noticed disabled people using burros and donkeys as crutches to make their way through the streets. And if one person can be credited with elevating the idea of a dog from man's best friend to man's essential service partner, it is Bonnie Bergin. In the world of Assistance Dogs, Bergin is renowned as a combination Madame Curie and Henry Ford.

Though references to dogs assisting blind people can be found in literature as far back as the early Middle Ages, it was not until the late 1920s and early 1930s that the first Seeing Eye Dog training schools were opened in the United States. Americans borrowed the concept from an institution in Germany that ministered specifically to veterans blinded during World War I. German Shepherd puppies were identified early on as the go-to dog for the purpose, although a good 45 percent of them washed out of the programs due to physical ailments or temperament, and that percentage remains about the same today.

Coincidentally, it was also during World War I that an American soldier named Lee Duncan rescued a German Shepherd puppy from a bombed-out kennel in Lorraine, France. He named the emaciated pup after a small puppet that French children had handed out to American doughboys disembarking in Europe. Duncan later wrote that the animal so lifted the spirits of his unit as they fought across the Western Front that there was never a question of abandoning him at war's end. Thus, prior to his movie career, Rin Tin Tin may well have been the US Army's first psychological Service Dog.

Unfortunately, for the next half century, Rin Tin Tin was also its only one, as the concept of Service Dogs was limited strictly to Seeing Eye Dogs—and even that idea took a winding road to catch on. It began in the wake of the Great War, when the first formal guide dog school opened in Potsdam, just outside of Berlin. It closed soon after due to a lack of funds in depression-ravaged Weimar Germany, but not before a Philadelphia socialite living in Switzerland named Dorothy Harrison Eustis learned of the program, toured the facility, and studied its curriculum. Eustis, intrigued by the idea of guide dogs assisting America's blind, wrote a story about her visit to the Potsdam school for the *Saturday Evening Post*.

Her article in turn prompted a young blind piano tuner from Tennessee named Morris Frank to write to her requesting a guide dog. Eustis replied that if Frank would come to Switzerland, she would train a dog for him. Frank, from a wealthy family, did just that and promised Eustis that when he got back to America, he would begin his own guide dog program. He kept his promise, returning to Nashville with his pioneer guide dog, Buddy, a German Shepherd, and incorporating the nation's first guide dog school in 1929. Frank named the institution the Seeing Eye after a verse from Proverbs: "The hearing ear, and the seeing eye, the Lord hath made even both of them."

Two years later, Frank relocated his school to New Jersey, and an industry was born. He spent the next twenty-eight years traveling the country and Canada championing not only the benefits of Seeing Eye Dogs but also the rights of blind people to be accompanied by their dogs into places where animals had previously been banned, such as train cars and hotel rooms. Then in 1975, a mere forty-eight years after Frank posted his letter to Dorothy Eustis, a former English teacher named Bonnie Bergin founded the nonprofit Canine Companions for Independence, the nation's first Assistance Dog program, in Santa Rosa, California.

Bergin's concept was not met with universal acclaim. The

Seeing Eye Dog industry considered its dogs the supreme beings of the craft and tried to paint the upstart Assistance Dogs as unqualified, or even outright frauds. But as Bergin's program gained popularity —in particular among parents of disabled children—the guide dog industrial complex grudgingly accepted Assistance Dogs, albeit relegating them to the niche market of pulling the wheelchair-bound disabled up ramps and hills. Despite the resistance, however, Bergin slowly revolutionized the Assistance Dog industry. Her animals were trained to open doors, turn light switches on and off, and help the disabled to dress and undress.

During paws4people's infancy, Kyria even adopted the vernacular Bergin had coined for this new kind of animal—half service companion and half loving partner. She taught the p4p dogs the simple Bergin commands—such as "wait," "pull," and "tug" —and through a series of trials and errors with the children, she sensed that body language in both humans and animals was a key to matching them up. Years later this would result in paws4people's unique concept of allowing the Service Dogs to select their "owners" at a public presentation devised by Terry and Kyria, which they christened their dog-to-client "Bump."

The Bumps, which take place in one of the West Virginia penitentiaries where paws4prisons dogs are trained, are all-day affairs, and they are exercises in raw emotion. They begin with clients and their families being ushered into a large prison day room by Terry and Kyria, where from a podium they introduce themselves to a crowd that includes paws4people volunteers, inmate trainers, and various Bureau of Prison or West Virginia Division of Correction personnel. At Terry's insistence, the clients then detail their most intimate fears, hopes, and secrets—all the reasons they need and want an Assistance Dog. No sharing, no dog.

At Bumps I have witnessed hardened combat veterans break down as they spoke of the heartbreaking causes and effects of their PTSD symptoms and parents weeping over their sick or disabled sons and daughters as they recounted the litany of treatments, surgeries, and physical, emotional, and psychological wounds their kids have suffered. The clients and their families are not the only people shedding tears. By the time the recitations are finished, there is rarely a dry eye in the house. After these testimonies, the dogs in training are led to clients one by one. Terry and Kyria sit off to the side with a kind of scorecard to evaluate the compatibility they observe between human and animal. Rarely does a Service Dog not exhibit an attachment to its human client by the end of the day.

But the Bumps were all far off in the future as Kyria, like Bonnie Bergin decades earlier, honed her dog-training skills. Whereas Bergin had to volunteer at local California humane societies to get a feel for the animals, Kyria had her own burgeoning dog pound at her fingertips with Riley, Addie, Brielle, Oatley, and Brinkley.

Knowing the personality of her dogs so well made it easier to study individual IEPs in order to adapt the dogs to a child's needs. Pretty and athletic, Kyria continued with her other extracurricular activities, such as cheerleading, and her grades certainly did not suffer. But Terry recalled how "this dog business," as he put it, gradually took over his daughter's life. He wondered at the time from whom she had inherited this insatiable drive to help the less fortunate—and I wondered if he had forgotten about the time at Vanderbilt when he had stepped into the fray to aid the coeds being harassed.

As it was, to Terry's everlasting surprise, he soon discovered himself celebrating the grit of a young boy born with multiple sclerosis who was able to crawl through a makeshift tunnel with Addie by his side or a little girl's determination to overcome her learning disability by counting out the correct number of Froot Loops she was then allowed to feed to Brinkley.

"The dogs were like teachers," he said with audible wonder in his voice. "They could get these children to do what you and I might consider the simplest thing, but to these kids it was like climbing a mountain. Walking across a stretch of school property that begins as loose gravel, then turns into grass, which in turn becomes asphalt? No big deal? Not to an autistic child who might find the change in surfaces overwhelming. But put a leash in that child's hands and she becomes more consumed with having the dog than with the change from gravel to grass to asphalt. Voilà, off they'd go.

"Or take speech therapy classes. The children were so eager to please the dogs—not the human teachers—that we'd use the animals to teach them new words like 'sit' or 'stay' or 'down.' And when they got it right, when the dogs obeyed their commands, they were allowed to feed them a treat."

Now the recollections of those early years rushed at Terry in a torrent. He inched closer to the panting Claire as he described a little girl named Maisie, suffering from cerebral palsy, who took her first tentative steps with Addie at her side. Then there was Nicholas, born with brain damage. No matter how hard Nicholas tried, he could never make it through an entire recitation of the alphabet. Yet one day, clinging tight to Addie, he managed to make it from A to Z in the correct order. The celebration in the classroom was joyous, and Nicholas's reward was being allowed to pet and brush Addie's coat. After he finished, he wrapped his tiny arms around Terry's neck and hugged him. This gift, Nicholas said, was what kept him going through all the letters of the alphabet.

"He wouldn't let go," Terry said as his eyes took on a faraway look and a small smile peaked at the corners of his mouth. "He just kept thanking me and thanking me. And I'm saying, 'No, Nicholas, thank you. Thank you.' Keeping busy with these poor kids, I didn't have time for my own depression."

Word of mouth spread, particularly through parent-teacher conferences and PTA meetings, and by Kyria's senior year in high school, her and her father's dog therapy sessions had proven so successful that the Loudoun County School District officially incorporated them into its IEP programs. Terry was asked if he could handle nine elementary schools, forty-five classes per week. There was no pay, and it would mean quitting his job at the tele-communications firm. He said yes.

Terry wiped a tear from his eye with the sleeve of his blue Windbreaker and told me that all that was left to do in this rush of newfound possibility "was to come up with an official name for this . . . *thing* we were doing."

As luck would have it, one of their neighbors was a graphic artist who designed the organization's distinctive logo and helped Terry and Kyria, sixteen at the time, settle on the name paws4people.

"As young as she was, it was Kyria who provided the real impetus behind paws4people," Terry said. "She hung the canvas, and I think part of it's been painted by me and part of it's been painted by her."

Suddenly Claire let out a high-pitched yelp.

The dog lay on her side, and Terry scrambled to lift her top hind leg just as, at precisely two minutes past midnight, the first amniotic sac, a tiny blood-red balloon, rolled out of her birth canal.

Chapter Two

Emilia

Terry quickly slits the sac's thin membrane with a scalpel and lifts the inert, fist-size puppy toward Claire's mouth. Claire licks it furiously to stimulate its bloodflow to the lungs and other organs while Terry snips and ties off the umbilical cord with a hemostatic clamp just as the veterinarian taught him. He swathes the tiny ball of fur in a warm blue towel while continuing to hold it near Claire's face.

"It's a boy," he says with a huge grin, and his large hands gently massage the unmoving form. Claire continues her licking until the puppy finally starts to squirm and mewl. I am surprised by his thick, golden coat. I also did not expect the pup's eyes to be closed. "They stay blind for a couple of weeks or so," Terry says as I reach for the strips of yarn.

"What color first?"

"Well, a boy," Terry says. "Your choice. You're his godfather."

I select a length of black yarn and hand it to Terry, who ties it loosely around the puppy's nape and places him on a scale. "Kyria will name them," he says. "Probably not tonight. Within the next couple of days."

In fact, since Claire's initial litter three years earlier provided the first puppies trained for the paws4vets program, Kyria has taken to naming all of Claire's offspring after American forts and military bases. (This firstborn will soon be named Shaw, in honor of the US air base in South Carolina.) But for now, as I squat on the floor and Terry hands me the tiny living being, I eye the black collar of yarn and come up with my own name.

"Hello, sweet little Blackie," I coo.

He weighs exactly one pound, and given his shape, heft, and texture, I feel as if I am holding a hamster. I give him a final caress before I place him on the floor near his mother's belly and nudge him toward one of her eight teats. He might be blind, but the pup roots around with his tiny snout, burrowing in until he finds a teat. His mouth attaches for dear life. Claire is not yet producing milk, but the pup's suckling will kick-start the lactation process.

I watch transfixed, until Terry's voice snaps me out of my reverie.

"Think about it," he says. "Somewhere around two years from now, maybe less, this tiny little thing is going to be an Assistance Dog, helping to complete someone's life."

He caresses Claire and exhorts her to keep pushing. "When they're born," he adds, "I always wonder who they'll end up with."

"A child," I blurt out, perhaps a little too loud. Terry's head swivels and another smile creases his face. He's got me. I feel my cheeks redden and suddenly remember a line from Psalm 107, one of Terry's favorites.

Oh that men would praise the Lord for his goodness,
and for his wonderful works to the children of men!

"Just a gut feeling," I say, embarrassed. But I am remembering my visit to the home of Emilia Bartlinski. Long before I journeyed to North Carolina to witness Claire delivering her pups, I traveled to the leafy suburb of Catonsville, outside of Baltimore, to visit the incredible Bartlinski family.

In my months chronicling the works of paws4people, I have met many brave and extraordinary children and adolescents living with physical, psychological, neurological, and emotional disabilities. But if, as they say, you always remember your first most fondly, Emilia Bartlinski is that one for me.

<hr />

"God only puts hurdles in front of those He knows can clear them."

Ann Bartlinski reached out to run her fingers through Mayzie's thick, copper scruff, and the three-year-old Golden Retriever reacted with a soft growl.

"This dog came to us for a reason," Ann continued. "I am convinced it is all in God's plan."

She turned toward her daughter with a loving smile. "Isn't that right, Emilia? Don't you think it was God's love that brought us Mayzie?"

Nine-year-old Emilia Bartlinski, huddled nearly into the folds of her mother's blouse, threw a shy glance at the stranger sitting at her kitchen table on this soft summer morning. Her thick, raven hair framed her oval face down to her dimpled chin, and she wore bright, spangled sneakers, patterned jeans, and a Baltimore Ravens T-shirt.

"Yes," Emilia said in a nearly inaudible puff of breath. She wrapped her good arm, the arm not encased in the plaster cast, around Mayzie's neck and giggled. "Yes. I love God, and I love Mayzie, too."

With that, she began rubbing the soft folds beneath the dog's chin while Mayzie inched tighter into the embrace of the little girl's good arm.

At a glance, the Bartlinski home appeared to be a typical suburban enclave, down to the tree-lined cul-de-sac and the SUV parked in the toy-cluttered driveway. But the handicapped tag on the SUV's license plate was the first giveaway that conditions were not quite as idyllic as they seemed, as was the wheelchair ramp leading up to the front porch and the long blue hose that trailed from across the lawn and connected to an oxygen tank. Even the SUV's rear window, affixed with the decals of two adults, nine children, three dogs, and four cats, hinted that this was not your ordinary family.

Ann and Ed Bartlinski, a homemaker and a chiropractor, are the biological parents of four of those nine child "decals"—three tall and strapping boys now grown and out of the house and the blonde and lithe thirteen-year-old Grace, off this Saturday morning at lacrosse practice. And then there are the newcomers. To this day, the Bartlinskis are still not quite certain what they thought they were getting into when they decided to travel to China on multiple occasions to adopt five little girls afflicted with some of the worst birth defects known to humanity. What Ann and Ed *are* sure of is that even though all the world's ills cannot be healed in one fell swoop, it is their calling to try to heal them one child at a time. It certainly helps, Ann was quick to say, that Mayzie was along for the ride.

As Emilia, using Mayzie as a sort of living walker, limped unsteadily into the family room to join her sisters watching Saturday morning cartoons, Ann led me to her kitchen table and poured coffee. She explained that the scene I'd just witnessed began when she and Ed decided to accompany Ed's brother and his wife, as a show of support, on a journey to a Chinese orphanage. Her in-laws had no children of their own and had made arrangements to adopt a handicapped toddler. "Well, we had four healthy children," Ann said, "but when we got there and saw how these little orphan girls were treated as outcasts, just strapped to a chair or bed with a towel for a blanket and a weekly hose-down for a bath, it just seemed the right thing for us to do."

Ann is a tall, elegant woman, with cheekbones that could cut falling silk, and now she set her strong chin and unconsciously swept a wisp of blonde hair from her forehead. "Everyone wants to adopt a *normal* child," she said, throwing her hands up to form air quotes around the word. "The special needs kids never get chosen. Well, God said to take care of the orphans, didn't He?"

Ed and Ann had to cut through scads of red tape with the Chinese authorities—even remaining behind when Ed's brother and his wife returned to the States with their own adopted girl. But it helped that the orphanage was run by a Christian charity, and so at the conclusion of that first trip, the Bartlinskis returned to the United States with Mary, now ten, who had been born with a cleft palate.

Once back home, Mary underwent successful surgery to reconstruct her face. "It was such an emotional experience," Ann said, "that we felt we couldn't stop there."

Two years later, Ed and Ann made arrangements to return to the same orphanage—this time completing the paperwork beforehand—and found Lucy. As Ann put it, "Lucy has a little bit more special needs."

Indeed. Lucy, now nine but appearing much younger, was

born with a condition called dextrocardia—her heart is on the right side of her body—as well as congenital scoliosis in her neck and a disorder named Poland syndrome, a rare birth defect characterized by the absence of chest muscles. She is also missing one kidney and several ribs, and her lungs are so damaged that she suffers from severe asthma—hence the snaking oxygen tube I spotted on the front lawn. The girls had been playing outside just before I arrived.

As Ann served coffee and pineapple cake, Lucy sauntered into the kitchen in her purple-and-white Baltimore Ravens jersey—the Bartlinskis are all Ravens fans—the blue oxygen tube running from her nose and trailing across the floor behind her. Her head tilts slightly from the cervical fusion she underwent to treat her scoliosis, lending her a perpetually curious demeanor. This only increases when, as then, she flashes a big grin.

"Is somebody talking about me?" she said.

Her mother smiled back. "Somebody's talking about how you haven't picked your toys off your bedroom floor." Which sent Lucy scurrying off with a laugh.

On the Bartlinskis' third trip to China, they found Emilia and, as Ann recalled, it was "another love at first sight." Whether or not Emilia had been born with the bone disease called osteomyelitis, the Bartlinskis cannot say, although it is more likely she contracted it at the orphanage. The painful disease is caused by a bacteria that can enter the bone in several ways, often through scrapes and cuts that are left untreated, and eats away at the bone and marrow. In children and teens it most often affects the long bones of the arms and legs, but it is easily preventable by flushing out those cuts and scrapes. And even when contracted, if detected in time, osteomyelitis is highly curable. Most American children diagnosed with the infection recover completely following medical treatment.

But I happen to know a little about Chinese orphanages. Two years ago, my brother and sister-in-law traveled to China to adopt a twenty-month-old girl, and they described the conditions in which the orphans lived—and they were all girls—as horrific, if not dystopian. The children were shown no affection whatsoever, and the younger girls were rarely lifted out of squalid cribs packed together like animals in a factory farm. Their bedding consisted of a lone towel that was hosed down, like the children, once a week. My brother told me it took him and his wife several days to clean all the caked dirt and grime from my new niece's hair and skull.

Thus it did not surprise me when Ann said that by the time she and Ed met Emilia, her condition had become chronic, running rampant through her body and destroying all the long bones in the toddler's arms and legs.

"When we first brought her home, her legs were so mangled—she was missing her left knee completely—that she used to just kind of throw them backward over her shoulders and scoot around on her rump," Ann said. "The doctors here told us they'd have to amputate both her legs."

In a disarmingly modulated voice, Ann described these horrors and her and her husband's rejection of that first doctor's recommendation to amputate their new daughter's legs.

"So we found one physician, a miracle worker, who said he thought he could rebuild her limbs one at a time," she continued. "I've lost count of how many operations she's had. And her left leg still doesn't have a knee; the bones are fused straight. But Emilia's taught herself to ride her bike without bending her knee, and she doesn't let anything stop her."

With that I glanced into the family room and spotted Emilia, Mayzie still by her side, clambering off the couch to retrieve a

Nerf ball to toss to the dog. She moved with her legs stiff, with no bend at the knee, as if she were walking on stilts. But the fact that she moved at all, well, yes, I would have to agree with Ann's description of miraculous.

As Ann refilled our coffee mugs, I remained riveted by this grim litany of maladies. For somehow it remained obvious that despite all the hardship, the Bartlinski home was filled with hope, love, and an optimism borne of supreme faith. It was that faith, Ann told me, that spurred her and Ed to make yet another journey to China, from where they returned with the now-six-year-old Gemma—whose bone marrow does not produce enough red blood cells, requiring her to undergo constant blood transfusions in order to prevent her organs from failing—and teeny-tiny Teresa, nicknamed "Fang Fang," also six. Teresa was born with permanently damaged lungs and only half a heart that will require transplant surgery as soon as a matching donor is located.

"Teresa was terminal and unadoptable," Ann said. "No one wanted her, and we weren't even sure she'd live through the plane flight. We were in the process of bringing Gemma home, and we really thought, 'No, we can't do this.' But it turns out God provided a way."

Much of those incredible provisions have come in the form of donations the Bartlinskis have received from their local Catholic church and from school fundraisers. And when a local newspaper ran a feature about the family that mentioned the brutal financial strains Ann and Ed have faced—although their insurance company could not legally drop them, their premiums and deductibles have soared—the outpouring from their community was, as Ann described it, "miraculous." Donations, some anonymous, poured in, and even the girls' doctors as well as Mayzie's veterinarian began volunteering their services.

Through it all, Ann said, Ed's chiropractic practice has remained steady, and she has adapted to the logistics of caring for all of the girls' special needs. Moreover, their older sons visit often to play with the girls, and Grace has embraced her new role of big sister as if she were born to play it, fussing over the younger girls' hair styles and outfits. Their entire family, she added, views the arrival of their adopted daughters, and even of Mayzie, as an "opportunity" that has been presented to them by God.

Like Thomas Jefferson, I imagine that if there is a Supreme Being, He or She must be as reasonable and rational as the laws of physics that govern the visible universe. To that effect, the Bartlinskis and the circumstances of their adopted daughters went some distance toward restoring my faith in the essential goodness of most human beings, whether what this family sees as an "opportunity" is a result of divine providence or not. But this brought up an uncomfortable question that had been hanging over the conversation since I'd arrived. So with the girls all out of ear-shot, I could not help but ask Ann how she, her husband, and their biological children coped with the certainty that at least some of their adopted daughters will likely never live past their teens. "Terminal," she had called Teresa.

Ann looked me in the eyes and replied with the serenity of a monk.

"If we can give these girls two more years of life, four more years, eight more years, then it will be two or four or eight more years of life than they would have had in that orphanage. That, to us, makes it all worth it."

I was still taking in this answer when the front door swung open and Ed and his daughter Grace entered, only to be swarmed by a mass of Baltimore Raven–clad humanity. There were hugs all around, and when the commotion died down, introductions were

37

made. Grace flashed me a confident smile before asking her sisters if they wanted to play in her room and hear about practice. They followed her down the hallway like a row of ducklings. Then Ed, tall and handsome with a handshake that felt like a board covered in sandpaper, plopped down in the chair beside me.

"So," he said, "I suppose Ann's told you about our first plan?"

He must have read the confusion on my face, for he glanced at Ann and broke into a broad grin. "Plan A—kids out of the house, retire, move to Florida, live in peace. Or at least that was my Plan A. But what does God say about plans? Guess He had a better one."

Then Ed swept his arm to encompass the television room, which his tribe of girls had returned to occupy like an invading army. "Our priest told us that we're on the front lines," he said. "And we kind of like being there."

He paused before continuing. "Still, I sure didn't know what the heck I was getting into. But as Ann always says, the grace of God will sustain you. And the girls, not to mention Mayzie, have been nothing if not godsends."

Although the Bartlinskis were already the owners of two pet dogs—Annabelle the Boston Terrier and Spanky the half Shih-Tzu, half Poodle (or Shih-Poo)—Ann had long been mulling the idea of finding a mobility Service Dog for Emilia. Emilia's operations to lengthen and strengthen her stunted arm and leg bones—thirteen and counting—involve cutting open the bones diagonally, inserting metal pins and rods into them, and attaching the rods to an iron and aluminum device called an external fixator that must be rotated by millimeters each night in order to realign and "regrow" the bone. Three days before my visit, Emilia had a fixator removed from her left arm, and that arm would be bound by the cast for another six weeks while the bone stabilized. Then she would start the process all over again on another limb. Constantly burdened by heavy fixators and plaster casts, Emilia had a quite natural tendency, her mother said, "to turn into a couch potato in front of the television."

"I'd ask her to go outside and play with her sisters, but she just wouldn't move. So I thought a Service Dog would help her get some exercise. Throw the ball with it. Throw the Frisbee with it. After her leg operations she was always in a wheelchair, and I also figured that, well, at the very least a dog could lie in front of her to make sure she wouldn't roll down the street if I was tending to the other girls. That, and I felt she also might need a companion to help her get through all her surgeries."

At this Ed interjected with a hearty laugh, "So I'm thinking, with all the chaos and commotion we already have in our lives— nine kids, four cats, two dogs—yeah, sure, just what we need, another living, breathing thing to take care of."

Then he shot his wife another knowing look. "But Ann can be . . . let's call it, very persuasive."

Ann laughed off the comment and said that two years ago she happened across an Internet story about paws4people, and she and Ed began researching the organization. The more they learned about "p4p"—as most clients refer to it—the more they liked it. Most service dog organizations will not place their dogs with anyone under eighteen. But Terry and Kyria, with their experience with special needs children, think this policy is ridiculous.

As Ann put it, "Mayzie is not the Bartlinski family dog; she is Emilia Bartlinski's dog."

Moreover, Ed and Ann were particularly intrigued by the organization's unique concept of allowing each Service Dog to select its owner at the paws4people Bumps. Prior to discovering

Terry and Kyria's organization, Ann and Ed recalled having preliminary contacts with several other agencies in their search for a companion for Emilia. Said Ann, "They just basically take down your information, come back to tell you they've trained a dog, and then present it to you. The dog doesn't actually get to know the child. We thought that p4p's method of matching the dog to the person, actually letting the dog pick the person, was phenomenal."

Soon after Emilia's application was accepted by paws4people, Ann and Emilia drove to the Alderson Federal Prison Camp for females in the mountains of West Virginia for Emilia's fabled Bump. Ann described it as Emilia bounded back into the kitchen to hover between her mom and dad.

"They brought the first two dogs out one at a time," Ann said. "And neither would go near Emilia. She was in her wheelchair, and she was wearing her fixator around one of her legs. It looks like a big cage, and I think the dogs . . . "

"They were scared of me," Emilia blurted out as she held up her left arm, encased in a plaster cast, as if to explain.

"But then they brought Mayzie out," Ann said. "And she ran right over to Emilia and started sniffing her arm and her leg. Then she jumped up and put her paws on the armrest of the wheelchair and started giving Emilia big, wet kisses. She didn't have a fear in the world. It was incredible."

Even more incredible, perhaps, is that since being placed with Emilia, both of Mayzie's hip joints have developed severe arthritis. "It's just so ironic," Ann said. "A Service Dog with severe bone issues, and she chooses a child with severe bone issues. This dog is so intuitive; we wonder now if that had something to do with the way she and Emilia just immediately hit it off."

Following Emilia and Mayzie's Bump at Alderson, the dog

was transferred to West Virginia's Hazelton Federal Prison for additional customized training to meet Emilia's needs. The Hazelton penitentiary complex houses three separate prisons on one site, and Mayzie completed her training in the prison's female facility and its male minimum-security camp. Coincidentally, both Mayzie and a convicted white-collar felon named David Burry who worked as a trainer for p4p at Hazelton were released from the institute around the same time.

David credits p4p with helping to turn his life around in prison, and when he returned home to the Philadelphia area, he reached out to Terry and Kyria to volunteer his services as a trainer. It was David who introduced me to the Bartlinskis. More about those amazing particulars in due course, but for now suffice it to say that Terry took David up on his offer and requested that he draw up and supervise Mayzie's specialized Public Access training, tailored to conform specifically to Emilia's needs.

Mayzie lived with David for nearly seven months, and the two visited Emilia every week. The early lessons consisted of David teaching Emilia how to convey the same basic commands—"tug," "stay," "walk"—that Mayzie had learned in the prison. He also taught Emilia paws4people's "house rules." These included a list of simple commonsense regulations, such as never—ever—feed Mayzie table scraps, ensure that she gets her daily exercise, and always make certain that in public she wears her vest identifying her as an Assistance Dog.

Patience was the key virtue, and this proved a double-edged sword for Emilia. At the time, she was still relatively new to the English language, and learning to issue a clear and authoritative command to Mayzie proved challenging. In fact, she herself had to learn what some of the words meant. As David said, "In the beginning, Mayzie was so game, you could tell that she and Emilia had formed a strong emotional bond. But because of Emilia's soft voice and accent, the dog had very little idea what she was being asked to do."

Over time, however, Emilia came to realize the importance of a strong voice, expressive body language, and—most of all— exuding confidence in her commands. Then it was time to adapt Mayzie to Emilia's special needs. The dog learned, for instance, how to brace the sometimes-wobbly girl as she climbed up and down stairs; in effect, the dog acted as something of a second bannister. It was also drilled into Mayzie that though there may be a loving tribe of girls constantly underfoot, she was, and would always be, in Emilia's charge. David would have all the girls line up in the backyard and peel off one at a time. Mayzie was instructed time and again to only follow Emilia. Emilia was the only person in the family who walked and fed Mayzie, thus reinforcing the bond. Then, a few months before my visit, David dropped off Mayzie to live with the family.

"All the other sisters try to steal Mayzie, and Emilia certainly shares her with them all," Ann said with a chuckle. I looked at the girl and her dog. The animal glanced often around the room at the sound of the other girls' voices and giggles. But her eyes always returned to Emilia. Ann read my thoughts.

"Make no mistake," she said. "Mayzie is Emilia's dog."

From puppyhood Mayzie had proven a quick study and had shown an eagerness to learn, the key requirement for all paws4people Service Dogs. Yet after spending most of her early life in prisons, now it was time to take the next step, to be taught to ignore the multiple stimuli that most pet dogs take for granted. So David worked with Emilia and Mayzie in the Bartlinskis' yard to suppress the animal's overwhelming natural instincts to explore her new world. Using a combination of a leash and treats, for instance, David and Emilia taught Mayzie to ignore any other living creatures in the vicinity. Eventually not even Emilia's sisters, other neighborhood dogs, or even a darting squirrel or cat could draw the unleashed Mayzie from Emilia's side.

That being said, a familiar yard is one thing, a public park or downtown street quite another. To that end, David, Emilia, and Mayzie also practiced a dizzying range of Public Access tasks, including negotiating hundreds of revolving doors, learning when to walk or halt at intersections by observing the flow of pedestrian foot traffic, and becoming desensitized to passing vehicle traffic (a tractor trailer's air brakes can be a terrifying sound the first time a puppy hears them). These tasks were accomplished by subjecting Mayzie—again, first with a leash—to busy downtown intersections over and over and over.

Among the many new concepts Mayzie needed to get comfortable with were restaurant and elevator behavior. Each time Mayzie sat quietly under a table for the length of a meal, she would be rewarded with a treat and showered with hugs and praise. Similarly, for the elevator training, Mayzie would accompany Emilia into a relatively small, enclosed space for a short period of time and would be rewarded if she stayed perfectly still.

By the time Emilia and Mayzie were ready to venture out in public, the little girl knew exactly what to say when strangers stopped them on the street and asked to pet her dog—either "Yes, you may" or "No, I am sorry, my dog is working." Within weeks of her arrival, Mayzie had become a loving and integral part of the Bartlinski household. Ann described for me standing at her front window watching Mayzie "herd" her daughters around the cul-de-sac to ensure they did not wander too far from home.

At one point during my visit, the girls, led by Grace, came streaming through the kitchen and burst through the back door to play in the yard. Ed, Ann, and I meandered out onto the back deck of their home to watch. The dog leaned gently against Emilia's hip as the little girl used the bannister to slowly negotiate the flight of stairs leading down to the large swath of lawn. And though Mayzie showed a passing interest in the others as they tossed Frisbees and whiffle balls for more than an hour, she never strayed more than a few feet from Emilia's side.

At one point, all the girls except Emilia followed Grace to the back corner of the yard chasing a butterfly. Emilia plopped down on the bottom of the steps leading down from the deck, looked up at her parents, and said, "I'm just a little tired." I swear I could feel Mayzie's internal tug. The pet in her wanted, really wanted, to be across the yard with the others running and chasing that butterfly. But the Assistance Dog in her prevailed. She sat next to Emilia and laid her head in the girl's lap. Emilia fed her a treat and stroked her nape.

A smile creased Ed's face as he took in the scene. "Emilia and Mayzie, the two of them play outside all the time now," he said. "The mobility help, the physical side, it's been more than we could have expected. But what we didn't see coming is the emotional and psychological ties that have blossomed between the two."

Ann agreed that she has been surprised and delighted by the emotional comfort and confidence the dog has provided their daughter. Not only has Emilia's English improved substantially, Ann said, but Emilia now also exhibits a remarkable sociability and self-assurance in public settings, particularly in school. Mayzie's arrival has, both parents told me, managed to help their daughter break out of her deep shell.

Ed noted that when Mayzie visited Emilia's first grade classroom last year for Show-and-Tell Day, the dog's effect on Emilia's classmates was tangible. "Kids being kids, I think they were a little afraid of the girl who was different, who always had casts and cages on her body. But once they saw she had a dog and that the dog would obey her commands, it was suddenly, 'Oh, Emilia's cool.' She's just so much more confident with Mayzie by her side."

Then Ann nodded toward the two and said, "When we first brought Emilia over from China, she was, well, shy isn't the word; she was shut down. Everything she had gone through at the orphanage was like a wall that prevented her from bonding with us. But once Mayzie came into the picture, she blossomed. She talks to her, she brushes her, she feeds her, even picks up her poop. It's not only given her a responsibility, it's given her an opportunity to care deeply for another living thing that cares back for her. Emilia has taken to keeping a journal, and she writes about her 'best friend' Mayzie nonstop."

The Assistance Dog's beneficial effect has even persuaded Emilia's physicians to allow Mayzie to accompany Emilia into the hospital on her numerous appointments and checkups. They have also made special provisions to permit the dog to enter the operating and recovery rooms during Emilia's many surgeries. Mayzie, wearing a custom-made hospital gown, jumps up and snuggles with Emilia before and after each one. This is a particular comfort, said Ann, who for the first time all day appeared to be holding back tears as she described her little girl's courage.

"Emilia had a lot of emotional issues," she said. "And this dog has just helped her unbelievably. Psychologically, she can relate to the dog where she could not relate to us. Emilia couldn't express her emotions, if she was excited, if she was frightened. Now she talks to Mayzie about them. We can hear her in bed the night before a surgery whispering to Mayzie, telling her that she's scared."

Ann looked toward her husband. "She never did that with us."

Ann and Ed estimate that Emilia will need at least a dozen

more operations on her limbs, and their greatest fear is that Mayzie's bad hips might someday render her unsuitable as an Assistance Dog. For now, Mayzie undergoes physical therapy once a week—walking on an underwater treadmill—to strengthen the muscles around her hips, and Terry and Kyria have worked with the Bartlinskis to supply the dog with a series of supplements and a daily regimen of vitamins that will keep Mayzie pain free and active for as long as possible.

But the Bartlinskis have been told that it is likely Mayzie will one day need her own hip replacement surgery, which p4p will help pay for. If necessary, should Mayzie not be able to resume her duties, the organization will Bump Emilia with a second Service Dog. For now, everyone is keeping their fingers crossed.

"It could happen any time, jumping to catch a Frisbee, stepping off the curb wrong," said Ann, her voice trailing off.

Ed picked up the thought. "That dog, she doesn't show her pain because she's so stoic, but it's there. So much like Emilia."

From the bottom of the stairs Emilia's tiny voice chimed in. "I like hugging her," she peeped. "I like lying with her and holding her hand. And she likes laying her head on me."

Soon enough it was time to leave, and Ed escorted me through the front door. Midway down the driveway he stopped, stroked his chin, and said, "You know, when Ann calls Mayzie intuitive, she's really not kidding. That dog just has a sixth sense, not just about Emilia, not just about the girls, but about all of us. She was sent here for a reason. She really was."

As we spoke, I noticed that Emilia and Mayzie had trailed us out of the house. Mayzie looking eager and sharp in her customized Service Dog vest with its two water bottles—one for Emilia, one for the dog—snapped into the vest pockets with carabiners.

"I forgot to tell you something important," she said, glancing shyly from me to her dad to her dog. "If somebody's hurt or crying, Mayzie always comes to say hello and see if you're okay."

Can a heart break and soar simultaneously? I swear mine did as I watched Emilia, Mayzie beside her, wave me goodbye. Here was a young girl born into deprivation, swooped out of the only miserable life she had ever known, plopped down among strangers she was told were now her new family, and poked, prodded, and cut open by doctors who could offer no end in sight. And it was a dog that had provided the lifeline that helped get her through these emotional and physically debilitating trials.

As Emilia receded in the rearview mirror, I noticed that she kept her eyes peeled on me all the way down the block. Mayzie, on the other hand, never took her eyes off Emilia.

Chapter Three

The Cheerleader

Terry is worried. It has been nearly an hour since the first pup arrived, and Claire should have delivered the next one by now. More troubling, Claire has yet to expel Blackie's placenta.

Terry is on his knees, whispering in the dog's ear and stroking her scruff, when the paws4people volunteer Renee Johnson arrives. Renee, a former aircraft mechanic who lives nearby, has become the center's majordomo, volunteering for jobs ranging from filling out paperwork to ordering dog blankets. Renee has been diagnosed with PTSD and is herself a recipient of a p4p Assistance Dog, a Golden Retriever named Travis. She quickly settles Travis into the kennel room with the other animals before stepping into the whelping pen with a clean quilt to replace the soiled blanket beneath Claire.

Terry and Renee are discussing whether to wake the veterinarian when Kyria bounds through the front door. She pauses just long enough to give her father a quick hug before beelining toward the suckling pup. Her wide-set green eyes are aglow as she lifts the tiny animal and smothers him with kisses. Kyria's ponytail is the same shade of gold as Claire's pelt.

Meanwhile, Terry is still wearing a concerned look. He has been kneeling beside Claire, coaxing her to push, but at a little past 1:00 a.m., he rises and begins digging through his knapsack, finally pulling out his cell phone.

"She may need a C-section," he says. Then, pointedly, to Kyria, "I don't like that placenta not coming out."

Kyria frowns, nestles the pup back into Claire's belly, and sidles close to her dad. "Just another ten minutes," she says. "Then we'll call the vet."

Neither seems confident that Claire will meet the deadline. Kyria is in fact busy packing Claire's travel bag when, at precisely 1:16, a red amniotic sac shoots from Claire's birth canal. Terry breaks the sac to reveal another golden puppy while Claire expels two bloody placentas. Kyria begins toweling off the newborn, cooing all the while, and a palpable sense of relief settles over the room.

Terry clips and clamps the second pup's umbilical cord before announcing another male. Kyria will name him Bragg, after the North Carolina army installation. Unlike the firstborn sleepyhead Shaw, Bragg starts to squirm almost as soon as Claire's tongue begins licking him clean, and I hand Kyria a length of navy blue yarn to tie around his neck. Now both Shaw and Bragg lock onto Claire's teats. The two are suckling with tremendous vigor as Claire snaps her head back between her hind legs, gulps down the two placentas, and licks her hindquarters clean of blood.

I let out a low, barely audible, "Eeeww," and Terry cannot help but stifle a laugh. His mood has lightened considerably, and he explains that as gross as this may appear to the uninitiated, Claire's appetite is good news. The placentas, he says, not only provide a meal of almost pure protein that will help her maintain her strength during the birthing process, "but in the wild it could be the difference between life and death."

"The bigger the mess," Terry says, "the more predators it attracts. Don't you ever watch any nature documentaries? Remember, these guys were once wolves."

In fact, thanks to Alexandra Horowitz's delightful book *Inside of a Dog* (as well as a steady diet of Animal Planet documentaries), I have become fairly well versed in the behavioral adaptations and breeding techniques that enabled your yappy Toy Pekingese or cuddly Cocker Spaniel to evolve from the fearsome prehistoric carnivore *Canis lupus* that would eat you for dinner without a second thought.

Wolf packs roamed almost all of the earth's ecological zones—forests, steppes, savannas, snowscapes—long before nomadic bands of *Homo sapiens* began appearing within their territorial borders some tens of thousands of years ago. When these two-legged hunter-gatherers finally settled into fixed communities, they naturally produced piles of waste, particularly food waste, which attracted scavenging wolves.

"The most brazen among them may have overcome any fear of these new, naked human animals and begun feasting on the scraps pile," writes Horowitz, who describes these nascent canid-human encounters as "accidental" natural selection.

Over time, some courageous (or foolhardy) humans likely took in the cubs of loitering wolves as pets—or, in a pinch, as meat and clothing—and gradually discovered that aside from companionship, the animals also had practical uses. They were handy for cleansing vermin from grain storage areas, for instance, as well as acting as early warning systems against intruders. Succeeding generations of these proto-pets were bred to perform tasks ranging from leading hunts to herding domestic livestock.

Archeological evidence suggests that the domesticated dog separated from *Canis lupus* somewhere between ten thousand to fourteen thousand years ago, although some experts believe the subspecies *Canis lupus familiaris* may have evolved as much as one hundred thousand years earlier. Either way, the dog's rapid evolution—by contrast, it took two million years for *Homo habilis* to become *Homo sapiens*—demonstrates the animal's remarkable social and behavioral adjustment. Add at least ten more millennia of selected breeding to this journey and, voilà, the dire wolf that once terrified Ug the Caveman is now your neighbor's tiny, flat-nosed pug.

The study of canine emotions and sentience is still in its infancy, but animal behaviorists have recently advanced theories that a dog's communication skills with humans surpass those of any other beast. Dogs may not be as objectively intelligent as primates, such as monkeys and orangutans, or even other four-legged animals, such as pigs, yet they possess not only the capacity for abstract reasoning and thought but also the means to express those thoughts to us. At least such is the contention advanced by the husband-and-wife research science team of Brian Hare and Vanessa Woods in their book *The Genius of Dogs*.

"Dogs had independently evolved to be cognitively more similar to us than we were to our closest relatives, the primates," they write. "Dogs are geniuses in their ability to read our gestures. Their skills are similar to what we observe in infants."

That thesis, based on years of research that Hare conducted at Duke University's Canine Cognitive Center, is borne out by examples ranging from a fellow researcher's mutt Sofie—who can discern various symbols, such as a faucet or a dog bowl, on a special audio keyboard—to a Border Collie named Chaser, who some consider "the world's smartest dog." When Sofie is thirsty, for instance, she will often lick her lips, pant, and press down on the keyboard's faucet symbol for water, which in turn announces the word aloud. Chaser, meanwhile, has not only learned the names of more than one thousand objects, she is also able to distinguish them among categories such as "dog toys" (like rubber chew bones) and "nontoys" (like a leash).

Then there is the simple gesture of pointing. Dogs have been found to discern what humans are "thinking" by observing them point. For example, when two tennis balls are placed equidistant from a dog, a vast majority of the dogs will inevitably retrieve the ball a human is pointing to. Even chimpanzees do not recognize "the point."

Hare and Woods also conducted experiments with dogs that suggest that these animals not only comprehend abstractions such as pointing but are also able to apply that thought process to the world around them. In one, dogs were played recordings of their owners' voices and then shown either photographs of their owners or photographs of strangers. They studied the strangers much longer, as if puzzled by the discrepancy between voice and picture. "They could only form such an expectation— when they hear their owner's voice—if they also remember what their owner looks like," Hare and Woods write. "The dogs could be doing this only by making an inference."

This inferential reasoning dovetails with the groundbreaking canine studies published by Gregory Berns, a professor of neuro-economics at Emory University in Atlanta. A few years ago, Berns invented a homemade MRI machine specifically contoured for the animals that, he writes, allows him to decode a dog's thought process by directly studying the brain of a dog who has not been anesthetized—heretofore the usual modus operandi for subjecting an animal to magnetic resonance imaging. His experiments, focusing on a region near the brain stem shared by humans and canines called the caudate nucleus, showed that many of the same dopamine receptors in the caudate nucleus that activate certain desires in humans—for food, for affection, for safety—have parallel receptors in a dog's brain.

A canine's caudate receptors, Berns writes, became more active not only in response to hand signals indicating food but also in response to the smell of a familiar human who had returned after momentarily stepping out of the room. Like Hare and Woods, Berns argues that a dog's ability to experience positive emotions, such as love and attachment, gives it a sentience comparable to that of a human infant. Berns's wry conclusion: "Dogs are people, too."

A stretch? Perhaps. But even the most skeptical among us agree that dogs, whether working animals or household pets, have adapted to "play us like a violin," as John Homans confesses in his book, *What's a Dog For?* Homans, a magazine editor, owns a black Labrador mix named Stella. As he writes, "Stella hypnotizes me with her big brown eyes, making me forget her gleaming wolfish teeth and the notion that, as I've been told, she's a parasite."

Interestingly, across the ten thousand–year epoch during which dogs became man's best friend, they also acquired a trait that wolves to this day do not possess—they will look directly into our eyes. Thus, as I now scan the whelping room and meet Claire's own doleful brown-eyed stare, the notion of her prehistoric ancestors tearing me limb from limb seems unimaginable.

It is as if Kyria is reading my thoughts. With a sly tone to her voice she says, "So, Mr. Tough-Guy reporter: Are we having fun yet?"

———

At twenty-seven, Kyria Henry is a wisp of a woman whose boundless energy belies her pixielike stature. The twin peaks of her upper lip suggest (ironically enough) a sort of feline cockiness, abetted by an athletic build and cascading golden hair not much changed from her college days rooting on the West Virginia University Mountaineers basketball team from atop the cheerleading squad's human pyramid.

Kyria is involved with every aspect of the p4p operation, from fund-raising to budgeting to supervising the dog-training regimen. Along with Terry, she arranges veterinary visits as well as the acquisition of breeding stock. Meanwhile, she also tracks the progress of clients and applicants for Service Dogs and teaches four Assistance Dog training courses each semester at the University of North Carolina Wilmington, averaging about six hours per week in the classroom.

Such is her enthusiasm and charisma that once within her gravitational pull, chances are you will find yourself volunteering for a paws4people project before the words are out of your mouth. In short, she is more verb than personal pronoun.

And then there is her rather esoteric name.

In January 1986, Terry and Debbie were driving to work together the morning after the space shuttle *Challenger* broke apart on takeoff, killing all seven crew members on board. As they listened to the radio, a caller asked the DJ to play the then-popular Mr. Mister song "Kyrie"—pronounced keer-ee-ay—in honor of the deceased astronauts. (*Kyrie, eleison* means "Lord, have mercy" in Greek.) Terry and Debbie were so struck by the lyrics—particularly the haunting refrain, "Kyrie eleison, down the road that I must travel; Kyrie eleison, through the darkness of the night"—they decided then and there on the name should they ever have a baby girl. Kyria Lynn Henry was born a year and a half later.

"I'm not certain what Paw-Paw and Mi-Mi thought was going through my parents' minds," Kyria told me when I joined her and her grandparents for lunch a few days before Claire went into labor. "But they eventually got used to the name. Maybe before they got used to me."

Jim and Pat Henry—Paw-Paw and Mi-Mi—had recently followed Terry and Kyria from Virginia to North Carolina, and they were still settling into their new home when Kyria and I met them for lunch at an outdoor café in Wilmington. It was a gorgeous, sun-dappled autumn afternoon, picture perfect for kicking back at a picnic table with trays of burgers and fries.

"Kyria was always, shall we say, a couple of years older than her true age . . . or at least acted that way," said Jim, a tall, handsome eighty-year-old with a nimbus of white, fleecy hair topping his ruddy face. "We used to marvel at her precocity. Everybody she came in contact with, well, let's just say that she was always the boss."

Added Pat, "Even when she was just a teeny-tiny sprig, she always had projects going. She'd get all the local kids involved in neighborhood clean-up days or the Girl Scout cookie drives. She and her friends used to put on plays for the families, make costumes, sell tickets, the works. Of course, Kyria was always the lead role."

One look at Pat Henry's broad, pleasant face, and it is obvious whom Terry took after. They both have the same pug nose. And though hobbled by near-crippling arthritis in her knees, back, and shoulders to the point where she often uses a wheelchair, Pat felt strong enough on this day to forgo the conveyance. As she dipped a french fry into a mound of ketchup, Pat told me that years ago, while Terry and his wife were at work, she and Jim would babysit their granddaughter. They weren't quite sure what to make of the little girl who agonized over receiving grades lower than A-plus, who spent hours practicing her penmanship, and who stomped and pouted when she didn't get her way.

Kyria's face turned beet red when Pat brought up the little black rocking chair they stationed in a corner of their living room to serve as Kyria's "time-out" seat.

"She spent a lot of time in that corner," Pat recalled with a chuckle.

"Amen to that," offered Jim with a big smile. I turned for Kyria's reaction.

"Guilty," she said through a sheepish grin "I don't even know how to describe myself without sounding like a control freak."

I found this discussion of Kyria's past all the more astonishing considering what I'd witnessed earlier in the day. Terry had recently returned from Hazelton Federal Prison with four new dogs, three Golden Retrievers and a black Labrador ranging in age from fourteen to twenty months. They had completed their rudimentary training courses, and Kyria had spent the morning testing them on the more than one hundred commands they had learned at the prison facility and sussing out their strengths and weaknesses.

One at a time she had led them into the huge, three-car garage behind the p4p headquarters and put them through their paces. First they were required to retrieve all kinds of objects—from plastic bottles of water to knapsacks to books—that she had placed around the floor of the garage. The Lab, first up, took naturally to this task, waiting patiently by Kyria's side until she gave the order to "fetch water bottle" or "fetch book" while pointing to the object. He bounded to the first object she vocalized, picked it up between his teeth, returned to Kyria, and held it gently in his mouth until she took it from him. He then sat by her side awaiting her next fetch command.

I got the sense that the Retrievers, unleashed and sitting in a row behind her with preternatural patience, had studied the Labrador's act. The first two performed just as well. But the third, the youngest at fourteen months old, was too full of enthusiasm. He tried to pick up as many objects as possible on his first "run," succeeding only in dropping one from his mouth when he scurried to the next. It was almost comical how much the confused dog wanted to please. Even Kyria laughed.

Instead of scolding the animal, she called him back, got down on her knees, gently grabbed the dog with both hands on each side of his head behind his ears, and looked him in the eyes. In a soft, modulated voice, she admonished him for not performing up to her expectations. She then stood, took hold of his collar, said in a strong voice, "Fetch water bottle," and walked the dog to the water bottle. When the Retriever picked it up, she walked him back to where they had begun while still holding his collar. She repeated this lesson with every object while the other dogs looked on silently.

When it was time to start the lesson anew, she again let the other dogs go ahead of the youngster. When his turn finally came, he was outstanding, bringing home every object she asked for. When she had taken the last one, the knapsack, from his mouth, she showered him with affectionate hugs, kisses, and caresses and rewarded him with a treat from a fanny pack brimming with Froot Loops. At a wave of her hand, the other dogs joined the group hug to receive their own treats. Kyria seemed to enjoy, if not revel in, their slobbering kisses. And then it was back to business.

While the dogs waited, I helped her form an obstacle course of plastic garden chairs. When we were finished, she leashed the dogs and had each pull her along the course in a wheelchair. Then they did it again, and a third time. All success!

The next task was not so easy. Kyria herded all four back inside p4p headquarters and asked me to leave the garage and observe through a back window. Then she brought the Lab back out. She ordered him to heel and sit, looked him in the eye, wagged her finger, and told him not to move. Then she walked out through the garage's open doors and disappeared around the corner. He looked a little antsy, his butt rising almost imperceptibly from the floor on a couple of occasions, but he did not move.

A few minutes later, when Kyria reappeared, he still did not move until she was standing right above him and waived him up. He jumped for a treat, and she led him back into the main hall.

All of the Retrievers had a harder time with this exercise, but most especially the youngest (again). While the two older dogs stood several times and whined and mewled, they managed to remain on the spot where Kyria had left them. Not the fourteen-month-old, though. The first time Kyria disappeared, as soon as she was out of sight, he dropped on his belly and began inching in a crawl toward the door like an infantryman approaching a foxhole. It was as if he knew exactly what he should *not* be doing, but his anxiety at being left alone nevertheless got the best of him.

Kyria had been relying on me to tell her how the dogs acted while she was out of sight, and when I informed her of the results, she once again ran through her gentle head-holding, eye-gazing castigation routine. By the third time or so, the two older Retrievers were sitting stone-still awaiting her return. It took the youngest dog a good half-dozen exercises, but finally he learned to sit alone like a statue, too.

Now that Kyria was finally satisfied, it was time for more wet kisses and treats.

It was repetitive and tiring work, but throughout the hours of these exercises, Kyria never showed any sign of visible frustration; not once did she raise her voice in anger or even turn her back on her charges to roll her eyes.

"We'll come back out this afternoon and do it again," she'd told me. "And tomorrow morning and tomorrow afternoon. For as long as we have to. Terry and I have a pretty good idea what applicants we'd like to place each of these guys with. They'll eventually be handed off to my students for even more honing to match the needs of those clients. But not before I am personally satisfied that they're ready."

She mentioned that her initial reading on the young Retriever was that he would never make it as a full-fledged psychological Service Dog or even a physical Service Dog.

"But I've been wrong before," she added, "plus, well, the world needs Social Therapy Dogs, too. No shame in helping kids learn to read or visiting soldiers in hospitals."

Still, I could sense she was disappointed. But then her mood brightened. "Did you notice how the black Lab was the best fetcher, a natural?" she asked.

I had. Toward the end of the fetching exercise with the Lab, she was not even using her finger to point, but merely jutting her chin before the dog would race to the object.

"He brought to me everything I asked for with no hesitation," she said. "We have a physically disabled soldier on our potential client list who needs help retrieving everything from his car keys to his clothes to his meds. I'm thinking of the Lab for him."

She then put out water bowls for all the dogs, and I assumed that we were off to lunch. But she suggested I head off to the restaurant, and she and her grandparents would meet me there soon. She had, she said, one more chore to accomplish. Instead I followed her back into the headquarters. She led the dogs into the kennel, removed her sweater, kneeled down on the floor, and began rolling around them all in one big, happy dog pile.

Her voice came out of the writhing mass of fur. "My favorite part of the job," she said as one of the Golden Retrievers ran his tongue up her face, leaving a gobby smear.

I stood off to the side watching. I was in shorts and not long before had scraped my leg, a small scrape, playing tennis. Suddenly one of the Retrievers carved away from Kyria and approached me tentatively. When I put out my hand to ruffle its scruff, it began licking the scab on my shin. I found out later that dogs do that to increase circulation and, in turn, boost the healing process.

Kyria was nine years old when her parents brought home her first puppy from a local breeder, the Golden Retriever she named Riley. "I was so happy because he was the prettiest, and I was sure I got the best of the litter," she told me.

As it happened, no one in the Henry family had any idea that Riley was the alpha dog of that litter, and Kyria's transition from pet owner to dog whisperer was not quite as smooth as Terry had earlier let on. She recounted how the "hard-headed" Riley would barely acknowledge her, much less obey her commands, and she recalled with a laugh the shivering winter nights she spent in the backyard waiting for him to do his business.

"He would just keep me out there in the rain, in the snow blowing sideways, eating grass or rolling in poop for as long as he darn well pleased."

Finally, when Riley was a few months old, Terry insisted that Kyria enroll him in obedience school. He had subtly put the onus of the dog's transformation into her hands. It was, Kyria remembered, a slow, tedious, two-year education for both of them, involving choke chains and prong collars as well as pockets full of treats. Slowly she deduced that the animal reacted much more fervently to positive rather than negative reinforcements, and in time Riley was responding so well to even Kyria's silent commands, issued through her body language and hand signals, that she felt she had "earned" the right to another dog.

"That's how I put it to Dad and Mom," she recalled. "'Hey, I successfully trained Riley. I deserve another one.' Plus, I wanted girls."

The female Golden Retrievers Brielle and Oatley, purchased from the same breeder, arrived in the Henry household next, followed shortly by another female, Addie. By two years later, when she and Terry decided to keep the female Brinkley out of the litter produced by Riley and Brielle, the entire family had taken notice of what Kyria's grandfather Jim called "just her natural gift of relating to these dogs."

Such observations went both ways, for it was also around this time that Kyria began to sense how her pets' presence would subtly lift her grandparents' moods. Jim in particular seemed to be frustrated in his retirement, blue about having nothing to work on, but when Kyria and her menagerie arrived, his face always brightened as he petted and wrestled with the dogs. Jim and Pat felt that caring for a full-time pet would be too much of a burden at their age. But during their granddaughter's visits they enjoyed playing with the dogs so much, Kyria remembered, "That I got to thinking, why not spread this joy? I didn't know much about Assistance Dogs. But I knew from the time we brought in Brielle and Oatley and Addie that they would be working dogs. Just working at what, I wasn't sure."

In 1999, at the age of twelve, she located an organization in Loudoun County that administered dog aptitude tests and, if the animals passed, awarded them Therapy Dog certificates. Her parents were skeptical. But after all of her pets received "diplomas," Kyria finally talked her father into chauffeuring her and the dogs to the local nursing homes and geriatric hospitals. By the time she was a sophomore in high school, not only were the dogs working full time with her and Terry, but she had also studied up on the difference between a Therapy Dog visiting hospitals or nursing homes for what she called pet-and grins and an actual working Service Dog.

At first these extracurricular activities were just another project that Kyria strived to excel at. But soon the project took a more gratifying turn.

"It was just the most fun, rewarding work," she said. "And to this day and age, I continue to be astonished by the lack of progress in understanding people with different abilities, particularly kids."

Moreover, it began to anger both Terry and Kyria that people in and out of the Service Dog industry seemed more accepting of an adult with an Assistance Dog than a child. Why should that be? Why shouldn't children and adolescents have the same opportunity to depend on a custom-trained Assistance Dog to help them with their disabilities? This inequality was driven home as they became more familiar with IEPs, which measure the physical, cognitive, social, and speech developments of children with special needs against what is referred to as their typical peers.

Recalling one such classmate with a speech defect, Kyria's voice adopted a soothing tone, as if she had traveled back to high school and was addressing the girl. "'The dog is not quite understanding your commands. So let's see if we can work a little harder on the sound of those r's.'"

Now she snapped back to the present. "You pick a realistic goal to reach—real-life self-care skills, like learning to brush your own teeth, counting to one hundred, picking up something you dropped. And I loved it when I could help one of them hit that goal."

She cited another special needs student, a girl her own age who had been born with the neurological disease called Rett syndrome. The girl could barely speak or walk, and as is the habit of many afflicted with the syndrome, she would constantly wring her tiny hands together as if kneading dough.

"Her muscles were so tight that she couldn't even feed herself," Kyria said. "Particularly on her left side, her left arm and hand. So part of her IEP was left-hand usage. She loved to brush the dogs and feed them treats. But we would only allow her to do it with her left hand. By the end of the semester, she had improved her left-hand coordination so much that she met all of her IEP goals. I was so thrilled. And from that moment, I knew that's what I wanted to do with my life. I wanted the whole world to know how these dogs were capable of turning people's lives around."

So she began traveling that career path accompanied by those closest to her. Or as her grandmother Pat told me, "Oh, yes, she certainly dragged us into it."

In fact, Kyria's grandparents have been a part of the paws4people family since Pat began occasionally accompanying Terry and his dog Addie to the Loudoun County elementary school special needs classes.

"I couldn't understand it at first," Pat said. "Our son the engineer, now he's with dogs as a career? It wasn't until I got into really working with Terry at the schools—Oatley kind of became my dog by default as Terry became closer and closer with Addie—that I began to understand how important this was. For both the kids *and* my son's mental health."

It was impossible for Pat to ignore how Terry's PTSD symptoms had transformed her formerly garrulous boy—the captain of his high school baseball team who once yearned to fly navy fighter jets—into a meek, standoffish creature seemingly afraid to face the world. But now she was witnessing how these dogs, the dogs her granddaughter had introduced into their lives, were pulling Terry back from the brink.

She told me a story about visiting one special needs class of five boys born with Down syndrome. Two of the boys, she said, were completely nonverbal, either unwilling or unable to speak. Terry was determined to "fix that." It was as if a long-lost glint in his eyes had returned.

"Those boys loved, and I mean *loved*, our dogs," Pat recalled. "And by the end of the semester, Terry had used those dogs to teach them to sign complete sentences. *May I please pet Addie? May I please feed Oatley a treat?* I'm not sure what was more striking, the change in those boys or the change in Terry."

Though Jim rarely went along on these early school sessions, he did volunteer to help out with the organization's bookkeeping, which he continues to do to this day. Meanwhile, by her sophomore year in college, Kyria had found a nearby elementary school in Morgantown with special needs classes. She began visiting the classes once a week with her latest pet—the Golden Retriever Bradie Lynn, Assistance Dog number six. She also convinced her roommate to join her, and the two incorporated the sessions into a philanthropic program sponsored by West Virginia University (WVU) called the Center for Civic Engagement.

After graduating from WVU, she devised a curriculum and syllabus for a university-level Assistance Dog program and worked with the administration at the University of North Carolina Wilmington to create a certificate program of four courses in the institute's College of Health and Human Services, School of Health and Applied Human Sciences, and Department of Recreation Therapy. She currently teaches some seventy to one hundred students per semester. Meanwhile, it took her a mere nine months to earn her master of arts degree from Liberty University in Lynchburg, Virginia, in human services: marriage and family counseling.

Married now for sixty years, Jim and Pat debated the merits of ordering the Oreo cookie ice cream versus the cherry pie for desert while telling me that they often reflect on the vagaries of life's ups and downs as they pertain to both their son and their granddaughter—although, as Pat pointed out, some things never do change, like Kyria's overwhelming drive for perfectionism.

"She wept when she came home from college once with a B in some subject," said Pat. "The only course in her life she got less than an A."

What sounds like a doting grandmother's praise is actually something of an understatement. In 2009 Kyria graduated from WVU with a bachelor of multidisciplinary studies degree in business administration, religious studies, speech pathology, and audiology. Of her 3.94 grade point average, she said with some heat, "That one lousy B really killed me." She was not joking.

When she is not teaching and cuddling with her dogs, one of Kyria's primary missions in life is to widen the scope of education about "the limitless world of Assistance Dogs." Like every project she tackles, she is a crusader on the subject, a distaff Don Quixote tilting her lance in particular against the countless grifters who lurk in the shadows of the Service Dog industry.

"There have always been con artists willing to use bogus Assistance Dogs to make a buck off someone else's misery," she explained to me, adding that they really began to emerge with the passage in 1990 of the Americans with Disabilities Act. However well-intentioned that law, its rules designating what is, and what is not, an Assistance Dog are notoriously opaque and open to so much interpretation as to make the matter moot. Further, and perhaps more important, there are no unifying federal or state governing bodies to mandate exactly what constitutes a certified Assistance Dog trainer. This confusion, combined with HIPPA regulations that forbid anyone from asking the owner of an animal purporting to be an Assistance Dog for paperwork, or even proper identification, has turned the industry into what Kyria called "the Wild West."

She noted that only a week earlier, on a short flight home from visiting p4p volunteers in Virginia, she noticed a "Service Dog Kit" on sale for two hundred dollars in the *SkyMall* magazine.

"It came with a vest, paperwork, and a form letter for your doctor to sign attesting that you require Service Dog assistance," she said, her voice rising in anger. "Some well-meaning physician who really doesn't know anything about, say, psychological Service Dogs but has heard good things about them signs off, and you're good to go. The law states your dog has to be registered with the Service Dog Registry of America. So we went online to see what that is, to download the application. All it requires is one witness to attest that your dog has never become aggressive. Send in that registration along with forty dollars, and your name's on the registry. Are you kidding me?"

Meanwhile, as more and more servicemen and -women return from overseas deployments with psychological and emotional disabilities, the sleazy tactics have peaked. The grieving families of soldiers and veterans suffering from PTSD and traumatic brain injury prove easy prey. Fake Assistance Dog purveyors approach these distressed moms, dads, wives, and husbands with wild claims about their animals' emotional healing powers, and in some cases charge up to $25,000 to deliver an untrained dog picked up at a local shelter. Naturally, when things go south—as they regularly do—the "Assistance Dog" suppliers are nowhere to be found.

Recently, after one such fraudulent dog, a German Shepherd, mauled a child to death on a Kentucky army base, the Department of Defense banned Assistance Dogs from the premises of all its military installations. Thus, the paws4vets pilot program at Georgia's Fort Stewart met its ignominious conclusion.

"Might be just as well," Kyria said with a weary frown. "I'm sorry for those soldiers. Terry was making so much progress. But I'm not sending my dogs, who we've spent thousands of dollars training, onto any base to be bitten by untrained dogs who came out of a shelter a couple of days ago."

Kyria also casts a chary eye on several of the giant Assistance Dog outfits that churn out unqualified animals by the hundreds. "Industrial dog factories," she called them, and she explained how they certify their animals as Assistance Dogs after training stints as brief as two days. Her concern is as much for the animals as for the humans with whom they are placed.

"Many of these large organizations who breed and place several hundred dogs per year have a graduation rate around 40 percent," she said. "If the dog does one thing wrong or has what they feel is one personality flaw or a medical condition as minute as an ear infection, it's gone. Sold as a pet. When I saw some of these systems firsthand, I decided that we'd take a different approach. Rather than placing them as pets, we'd work to find other Assistance Dog services for them to work at. We work really hard at finding alternative placements."

Naturally, these larger suppliers, even the legitimate outfits, find their systems more cost efficient. They can afford to. Terry and Kyria do not have that luxury. Thus in honing their training regimen, they have cherry-picked what they consider the most efficient aspects of dozens of Assistance Dog training theories and added their own through trial and error. At an average cost of about $35,000 per dog, it is not an inexpensive venture.

"We put too much effort into training our dogs," Kyria said of the more than three hundred animals who have passed through the p4p process. "And if we don't think one of them will cut it as, say, a psychological Service Dog paired with a vet suffering from PTSD, then we might try to train the animal as a mobility Service Dog paired with someone suffering from a physical condition who needs help with anything from being steadied as he stands or walks to having his wheelchair pulled up a ramp.

"And even though we don't specifically train our dogs for it, we've found that some are natural seizure-predicting and seizure-response animals. But even if one of our dogs doesn't meet any of that criteria, then perhaps she can work in our paws4education program visiting schools to help kids learn to read or as a Social Therapy Dog going to nursing homes and hospices and hospitals."

Some dogs, predominantly rescue mutts, just don't fit any of those categories. Usually these animals have been too physically battered or emotionally scarred—in many cases the two go hand in hand—to be of much use to anyone in need of an Assistance Dog. But, as Terry once told me, "I've never met a dog that can't be rehabilitated. It takes time and lots and lots of loving care, brainwashing the old, bad stuff away in a sense. It can be a pain, but it can be done."

To that end, paws4people will train its most challenging animals to become what Kyria and Terry refer to as Community Dogs, which they donate as pets to applicants who fit certain criteria, such as the spouse-less elderly. Their paws4seniors program, for example, caters to just these types of applicants. Terry can cite several scientific studies that posit that owning a dog will keep a senior's blood pressure levels within a healthy range and even increases the recovery rates of the elderly suffering from heart disease. Yet such "untrainable" animals are the rarities, and only four of the hundreds of dogs that have passed through the p4p pipeline have gone that route.

"And of those, all four were rescue dogs that came to us with too much baggage," Kyria said. "I guess what I'm saying is that there will always be somewhere for our dogs to be placed, to work to help people. Think of our training as a school for higher education. Unlike at the big dog factories, there are a variety of courses to choose from. It's not like, fail chemistry, you're out. We have multiple majors. Dogs are like people. They don't all want to do the same job. They don't all want to work with a disabled child or a marine with a psychological syndrome. We acknowledge that. So you flunk chemistry at paws4people, we'll enroll you in English lit or history or geology. Believe me, we'll find something you're good at."

Lunch was over, and by the time we had wiped our plates clean and bussed the picnic table, the sun had sunk behind a tall, elegant live oak towering over the restaurant's patio. Nearing the parking lot, Kyria suddenly stopped short.

"You know," she said, glancing at me, then to her grandparents, and then back to me. "It seems a fairly simple and straightforward philosophy to me. Working dogs, Assistance Dogs, make the world a better place. In fact, I'd even go so far as to say they can change the world. Who the heck wouldn't want to devote their life to changing the world?"

Chapter Four

The Slammer (1)

2:34 a.m. Another crisis. A partial amniotic sac emerges from Claire's birth canal only to disappear back inside the dog. It resembles a fire red balloon being blown up and then suddenly deflating.

"Bag crowned," Terry says. There is a hint of tremolo to his voice. "I think it's a breech. Man, what is going on tonight?"

He reaches for his phone and looks at Kyria. "The vet?"

Before she can answer, the amniotic sac reappears, again begins to "deflate," but then tumbles out onto the blanket in its entirety. Terry gently tears it open to examine the animal inside, then checks Claire's cervix for damage.

"It's okay," he says. Relief in his tone now. "She turned it around."

This pup needs no stimulating massage from any humans—it wobbles from the sac fully conscious—though Claire's licking ritual begins apace. Puppy number three is another male, soon to be named Lawson, and I am about to hand Terry a length of dark green yarn when he thrusts the tiny creature into my arms and spins back toward Claire.

"Can you tie on this one yourself?" he says. "Another on the way."

How he sensed this, I have no idea. But sure enough, at 2:44 as I cradle Lawson, a fourth sac bursts from Claire and breaks apart on its own in the process of delivering Harrison into the world. Yet *another* male.

Claire's first three deliveries have all been some shade of yellowish gold, with Bragg's coat the darkest and Lawson's verging on near white. But Harrison sports a deep golden fur, almost incandescent, and his tiny ears are the floppiest of the litter so far. He is also, to this point, the heaviest, at just over a pound and a half. As he joins his brothers fighting for a position at Claire's belly, I notice automobile headlights through the window and hear tires crunching along the center's gravel driveway.

A moment later, three of Kyria's university students walk through the front door. Savannah, David, and Mallory are enrolled in Kyria's most advanced Assistance Dog class at the University of North Carolina Wilmington, and she has apparently taught them well: Savannah is toting two large bags of McDonald's Quarter Pounders while David carries a cardboard tray laden with sodas.

Savannah tells me that she is a psychology major who one day hopes to incorporate Assistance Dogs into her practice, while David admits that he signed up for Kyria's course because he smelled "an easy A." He has, he says, since fallen for the world of Service Dogs. He's a natural with the animals, he has found, and is trying to figure out a career path that will include working with them. Mallory, a sophomore, is leaning toward enlisting in the navy after graduation and becoming a medical corps officer, but for now she finds that the Assistance Dog class, which enables her to work with both the dogs and p4p's clients, is her most emotionally and spiritually fulfilling course.

A huge smile bisects Terry's face as he watches the girls

immediately melt over the pups. They take turns shifting the four puppies around Claire's belly, surreptitiously sneaking in a quick cuddle before making certain each newborn has a clear path to a teat. Terry's eyes meet mine and he shoots me a knowing grin as he sidles up next to me.

"People think we only train the dogs," he says, and juts his chin toward the college kids. "But, you know, we also train humans. Train them how to train these puppies to be Assistance Dogs."

Early on in this journey, back at Fort Stewart, Terry had described for me the difference between a Direct Service Dog— one who is placed to live with a specific vetted client—and an Indirect Service Dog, who works alongside a professional, such as a therapist or a special needs classroom teacher.

"Those are generally the two categories, and naturally the dogs need to be trained differently," Terry says now. "You know why German Shepherds make such good Seeing Eye Dogs but lousy Service Dogs? Because there's something built into a Shepherd's DNA to form an almost unbreakable protective bond with its owner. That overprotectiveness works swell for a blind person, who more than most needs that tough bodyguard. But it doesn't work for our clients.

"Think about our clients. Kids. Vets with PTSD. Say one of them has an incident, a breakdown like Jeff in the PX. It happens more than you think with our people, as opposed to blind people. But a Shepherd wouldn't let people coming to Jeff's assistance— bystanders, friends, EMTs—near him. The dog would most likely have to be sedated. We can't have our dogs being shot with tranquilizer darts every time one of our clients has a breakdown."

"Yet," he adds, "there are different levels of that same strain of overprotectiveness running through most dogs, including p4p's Goldens and Labs and even our mutts." That's why Terry and

73

Kyria pay as much attention to the "doggie personality reports" they receive from the inmate trainers as they do to the training-task updates. The dogs that show a strong tendency to attach to one person are usually slated for the Direct Service Dog pipeline. Those that, as Terry puts it, "play well with others" are most likely to be assigned to therapists and special needs teachers who deal with myriad clients.

"So we also teach these kids the different nuances," Terry says, still smiling at the students fussing over the puppies. "The prison inmates, too. But the inmates, they're a whole separate deal."

He glances at Kyria, who has lifted Harrison from the pack and is passing him among her students. "Yep," he says, "you can thank my daughter for the inmates."

He is going for sarcastic, but I can hear the pride in his voice. And, indeed, were it not for Kyria's self-appointed mission to "change the world," there would be no paws4prisons program.

It began with Kyria's undergrad work with West Virginia University's philanthropic arm, the Center for Civic Engagement. She had familiarized herself with the school's prison outreach programs when, during her sophomore year, administrators from nearby Hazelton Federal Prison approached her about using the institution's recently opened female wing, and its inmates, as a training site for paws4people Service Dogs. Terry was skeptical. He had sent his daughter to college to earn a degree, not fool around with prisoners. Needless to say, Kyria prevailed, and she threw every spare moment into untangling the bureaucratic knot of paperwork the project required. That summer the West Virginia Bureau of Prisons signed on to the venture, although it was a closer-run gambit than Terry and Kyria knew at the time.

Kyria's government counterpart was the administrator of Hazelton's secure female facility, Susan Folk, currently an assistant warden at a Pennsylvania institution. Terry recalls meeting Susan for dinner several years after paws4prisons was up and running in Hazelton, and she told him that while evaluating the p4p application, she had sought counsel from her colleagues. Most were in favor of the idea of initiating a dog program in the new female wing—unfortunately, just not Terry and Kyria's. They suggested she instead contact a more established prison-dog program like Cell Dogs or NEADS, which provides Service Dogs for the deaf and disabled.

"At the time, our rescue dogs outnumbered our breeding stock," Terry remembers. "And Susan said her advisors considered us too risky, too new, too mom-and-pop. Then she told me, 'I prayed on it, and I came to the conclusion that Kyria and you were the right people for our program, and it's been proven a thousand times over.'"

Terry pauses. "Susan is one of the top five people in my life."

Over time, as Terry and Kyria contracted with breeders and acquired more puppies than Hazelton could handle, the paws4prison program expanded into four more state and federal penitentiaries throughout West Virginia. And though the inmate dog trainers remain predominantly female, the program has also made inroads into the men's prison population, particularly at Hazelton's minimum-security camp, where one of its first volunteers was none other than David Burry.

<hr />

You'll recall that it was David who accompanied me to the Bartlinski home in Maryland to introduce me to Emilia and her family. David now lives frugally in a rented apartment over a barn in an exurb of Philadelphia, and in preparation for our trip to

Maryland, we had made plans to meet at a rest stop on the Delaware Turnpike and drive the final leg together. When I pulled into the parking lot, I spotted a man pacing the sidewalk outside the Sbarro's and somehow instinctively sensed it was David.

David is tall and flagpole lean, with a tendency to enter and exit his car in the fashion of a praying mantis folding and unfolding his long legs. At fifty-four, his hangdog face is topped by a thick thatch of sandy hair beginning to gray at the temples, and his most prominent feature is a set of watery, pale-blue eyes that appear to be on the constant verge of weeping. Yet those big, sad eyes stand in contrast to his open and easy smile.

I was initially skeptical of Terry's and Kyria's reforming embrace of both current and former prison inmates like David. This was early in my research on the organization, and I carried the old reporter's caution: If something seems too good to be true, it usually is. David Burry proved me wrong. For as we felt each other out on our drive—who knows what he thought of this nosy reporter probing into the most personal corners of his life?—it did not take long before we had both let our guard down.

Moreover, David surprised me by recalling his years in prison as "an enlightening experience."

That threw me. Enlightening? In what sense? Again, the easy smile, now accompanied by a rueful chuckle.

"In the sense that while in prison, I discovered I was able to do something meaningful that would have the lasting effect of significantly benefiting someone besides me, someone in need. You'll meet a lot of people in this organization, the Bartlinskis among them, who will tell you that God has his reasons for everything. That's what I mean about an enlightening experience. When you're locked away, you get a lot of time for introspection. To think about how you can better yourself physically, mentally, and spiritually. I took advantage of that by taking vocational courses and working out whenever I could. Life, and God's overall plan for me, now seem much simpler and easier to understand."

Thirteen years ago, David pled guilty to three counts of bank fraud, mail fraud, and money laundering and was sentenced to twelve and one-half years behind bars. Prior to that, he had run a successful financial services business in the Philadelphia area and had seemingly had it all—a loving wife, an adoring son and daughter, a beautiful home, and a fine standing in his church and community.

But David was also a gambler, a small-time Gordon Gekko "taking advantage," he said with a shake of his head, "of every available business opportunity that crossed my path. I talked myself into believing that I and my family deserved everything we acquired. Greed and pride gradually eroded the godly values I had been brought up with. My life revolved around one thing and one thing only: the pursuit of money and pleasure. And then a single bad choice brought it all down."

The bad choice came in the form of a financial deal that turned sour. David had borrowed the money to invest in the venture from a business associate. Now he could not pay him back. He faced a choice: declare the truth or lie. He lied, fabricating another contract and accepting money from a second investor in order to pay back his original associate.

"I felt that I was facing humiliation," he said, "and my self-righteous pride wouldn't allow me to stand up and tell the truth. I felt that my integrity was at stake. I was just so myopic."

Unfortunately, his original lie necessitated more forged deals, and while running a classic Ponzi pyramid scheme, he found himself always scrambling to borrow from more and more Peters to pay off more and more Pauls. It took several years for the entire house of worthless paper to come crashing down on his head. By then, he owed investors more than $23 million.

The courts seized his home and all of his assets after his plea, and his devastated wife of twenty years divorced him. He entered prison broke and depressed, convinced that his life was over. Then one day, sitting at a table in the prison yard and wallowing in self-pity, an older prisoner whose financial crimes were remarkably similar to David's approached him out of the blue, handed him a cup of coffee, and said, "Prison has been one of the most enlightening experiences I've had in my life."

David didn't know whether to laugh or cry. How could losing everything and being separated from everyone you loved be a good thing for anyone? He was baffled—until his new friend advised him that his circumstances actually presented the chance to begin his life anew. David could not change the past. But he could certainly shape the future. And not only his own. Perhaps he could dedicate that future to helping others. Then his fellow prisoner mentioned that he might want to use his library-computer time to look into an outfit called paws4people.

The next day when he looked up the p4p Web site, he was immediately intrigued. He had always been a dog person—his family had kept several Golden Retrievers and Labradors as pets before his incarceration—and the idea of teaching an animal more than just to sit, roll over, or shake, of teaching it to open and close doors, to turn light switches on and off, to retrieve specific objects, fired his imagination. Most important, he would be teaching those dogs to work for other people, disabled children and veterans who needed them not as pets but as lifelines to society. *Helping others,* the old prisoner had said.

His wife may have given up on him, but he had kept in contact with his children, and he wrote to his teenage daughter, Ashley, requesting that she gather and send him any information on p4p that she could get her hands on. Soon thick manila envelopes filled with newspaper and printed Web stories chronicling p4p's birth and growth began arriving at the prison. His interest was naturally piqued when he read in the many profiles of Terry and Kyria that Kyria and his daughter were the same age. More important, he felt for the first time in a long time that he had found something to live for.

He requested an application, filled out all eight pages detailing his personal biography, and mailed it to Terry. A month later he was accepted into the program as an entry-level trainer. The first thing he did was memorize the 150-odd commands each p4p dog would have to master. Then, he remembered, one of his first and greatest challenges was an Afghan rescue dog named Sur who, unlike the majority of the eight- to ten-week-old pups entered into the paws4prisons program, had a lot of bad habits to break.

"A friend of Terry's had brought her back from Afghanistan, and for the first nine months of her life, Sur was just a wild dog living on the streets, no human supervision, no structure whatsoever," David said as we passed out of Delaware and into Maryland. "It took me months just to housebreak her, and another seven months after that—three to four times longer than it should have—to train her to complete the simplest tasks. I'm pretty sure Terry wanted to just boot her from the program. But I kept begging and begging. I wanted that challenge.

"I was down on my knees every day with that darn dog. Using my front *paws* to turn lights on and off. Retrieving objects with my teeth. Maybe she thought she was training me. In the end, Sur never did make it as a Service Dog; she ended up being the companion of a senior shut-in."

And here he emitted another small chuckle, as if reliving those days petitioning Terry to stay in Sur's corner. "But look, she's serving some kind of purpose. Even if it's just fetching someone's slippers. And I did that. Not for me. But for the dog and her new owner. It was the first time I was so passionate about something that would not benefit either me or my family. It felt good."

The dogs enrolled in the paws4prisons program live in the rooms or cells of each inmate, and David recalled that the program was not unanimously popular. He lived in a dormitory housing 120 fellow minimum-security prisoners—"no razor wire or anything like that, not the kind of place you see in the scary prison movies"—and some inmates initially objected to having to share their space with animals, either for religious reasons or just on general principle.

"Some plain just didn't like dogs, some were scared of them," he said. "But over time, as they watched what we did with these animals, I'd say the majority of the antidog inmates came around. It was funny to watch the loudest objectors eventually stop by asking if they could pet them.

"I know it sounds crazy—you're in prison, after all—but those are still some of my best memories. I could watch those dogs play and learn for hours, the way they communicated with each other with their eyes, their ears, their tails, their posture. The way they would express themselves with a sigh, a grunt, a moan, or a yelp. Seeing how happy they became when they discovered the association between the command and the act you're asking them to perform; that's called work-to-please.

"I'd never really thought about the diverse personalities dogs have. They were, you know, just dogs. But when you begin to study them as individuals, well, each one is unique. I found I could adjust my personality to complement theirs, and that made training them a lot easier. Heck, even when you weren't training, watching those dogs was better than anything on television in the dayroom."

In addition, he said, all paws4prisons trainers were—and are— expected to be conversant in disciplines as diverse as Assistance Dog wheelchair etiquette that is, where to stand in relation to either a moving or stationary wheelchair—to how to perform a canine physical exam to spot anything from ear infections to para- sites. Terry and Kyria periodically issue written tests to the inmates in these categories and more, and if they do not maintain a 90 per- cent grade point average, they are dropped from the program.

One key learning curve for inmates like David was under- standing how to modify behavior in "problem" dogs whose snap- ping and growling crossed the line from mere roughhousing during play time to actual aggression. A sharp "No mouth!" or "Quiet!" repeated over and over again usually did the trick. If not, well, David could only recall two dogs that had to be "flunked out" of the program.

After eighteen months with paws4prisons, Terry promoted David to lead trainer at the Hazelton camp, where he not only oversaw the project but also trained fourteen Assistance Dogs before his release almost three years ago. As Baltimore sped by outside our windshield, he named each one of them—as well as the eight more, including Mayzie, he had trained since. As he did so, his voice took on a reflective tone.

"There are times when we are faced with decisions that dra- matically change the course of our lives," he said. "This was one of those times, although I had no idea at the time that I was about to turn my world upside down."

Upon his release from Hazelton, David's daughter Ashley helped him find the barn apartment in the Brandywine Valley, not far from where she lives. And when Terry offered David a modest salary to head up a new project establishing pet-training centers at selected sites around the country—there are three so far, all on the East Coast, and their profits will redound to the nonprofit paws4people—he jumped at the chance. He is, he joked, delighted to be finally applying his business organizational and management skills to something "that's strictly legal."

Meanwhile, Ashley quit her job as a legal assistant, and she and her dad both also work as paws4people volunteers, traveling the Mid-Atlantic region to offer brush-up training and the annual Public Access tests that Terry and Kyria require of all the dogs they place. They also shuttle their own growing kennel of Assistance Dogs to Philadelphia-area schools with special needs classes as well as to local institutions housing troubled juveniles.

On our drive back from the Bartlinskis' home, David could not stress enough the comfort he takes in the fact that both Ashley and his thirty-two-year-old son Joshua have forgiven him his past mistakes. The three remain so close that Joshua has also begun volunteering his services to paws4people (his next project will be selling Christmas trees to benefit paws4vets). As we pulled next to my parked Jeep, David beamed while describing how Joshua and his daughter-in-law had "gifted" him with two grandsons.

"They're both still young, five and two, but we're already pretty sure they have a thing for dogs."

My day with David settled things. That night I called Terry to ask if I might accompany him on his next "prison run." I needed to personally witness at least a slice of the paws4prisons operation in action.

Not long afterward, I found myself driving nearly six hundred miles from New Jersey to the small industrial town of Gallipolis, Ohio, a long stone's toss across the Ohio River from West Virginia's brooding Lakin Correctional Center.

The sun had yet to rise on a frigid Monday in January when I met Terry in the parking lot of the Quality Inn in Gallipolis. He and his ever-present Chaeney had driven up from North Carolina the previous night with a litter of Golden Retriever pups birthed at the Wilmington center eight weeks earlier, and he looked haggard, the bags under his eyes the result of the long nights of caring for the newborns.

This was a healthy and handsome brood—their eyes clear and curious—and as I helped Terry load the gaggle of pups into the bed of his clunky, old gray Saturn SUV, I noticed the contrast between the friskiness of the animals and Terry's slow, measured movements. For the most part, the dogs were very well behaved for eight-week-olds, though it seemed to me that Terry became most animated when a few of them hesitated to jump into the truck on his first command and he was forced to raise his voice.

I thought of David Burry's comment about all dogs having individual personalities, and for the first time I considered these animals in a different light. Yes, of course, here was the shy one and the rambunctious one and the "licky" one and the one who appeared totally baffled by his new surroundings. I tried to pick out the alpha in the bunch, and though my eye was not yet trained enough to do that, I did notice that the smallest puppy, a light blonde beauty with a white blaze on her forehead, seemed as if she just wanted to hide in the farthest corner of the truck bed.

Terry had mapped out our itinerary with his usual military precision. Over the next two to three days, we would deliver the pups to the Lakin state penitentiary—or just plain "Lakin," as everyone refers to it—across the Ohio River and a few miles down the road in West Columbia, West Virginia, where they would settle in for several months of rudimentary obedience training.

From Lakin, we would transport three dogs who were ready to begin their next stage of training at the Alderson Federal Prison Camp, 180 miles away. And finally we would move four more dogs from Lakin to Hazelton Federal Prison, all the way across the state near the Maryland border. At Hazelton, Terry would load up three dogs who had recently "Bumped" with clients and were to begin their six to twelve months of Public Access training back in Wilmington. This involved, at the very least, twelve to sixteen hours of drive time back, forth, and back again across the mountainous state. We were lucky. The forecast called for overcast skies, but no snow.

Despite Kyria's best efforts to school me, I told Terry that I remained a little confused about where and how these different penitentiaries and work camps fit into the paws4prisons hierarchy. He admitted that the system was still a work in progress "and probably always will be." Where a dog trained, he said, sometimes depended upon which institution had room at the moment. He suggested that it might simplify things to think of Lakin as p4p's elementary school, Alderson as its middle school and high school, and Hazelton and the Prunytown Correctional Center, another state institution near Morgantown with a minimum-security men's camp, as its universities. The Wilmington center, he said, was analogous to a finishing school, where each Assistance Dog was groomed to respond to the specific needs of a client.

Moments later, as we crossed the majestic Silver Memorial Bridge spanning the Ohio River, I contemplated what was going through Terry's mind. He and Kyria, with help from Renee Johnson and Kyria's students, had lived virtually round the clock with these pups since their birth. Lakin would be merely their first stop along the paws4people "prison training pipeline," and by the time of their release from what Terry jokingly calls the slammer in twelve to sixteen months, they would be well on their way to being placed with a p4p client. Terry insists that the movement of p4p dogs like chess pieces around the eastern seaboard is simply a part of the business. But I could not help but wonder if his reserved demeanor had anything to do with having to say good-bye to—as he has referred to them more than once—his babies.

Perhaps it is not the most apt analogy, but the circumstance reminded me of the many times my son, Liam-Antoine, and I have parted company at the airport for what we both recognized would be long stretches of time. I've had what you might call a special kind of relationship with my boy since his mother took him back to her home country of France as an infant. She and I were never married, but I've always wished her nothing but the best; perhaps I'd just been the wrong man for her. Despite the complicated circumstances, one thing I've never stinted on is support for my boy—emotional, physical, and financial.

For the first five years of his life, before he could fly transatlantic by himself—at first with a flight attendant guardian, later on his own—I visited him often. I was traveling overseas a lot—a real lot—and wherever my reporting took me, I always made certain to fly home through France. Once, when he was three, Liam-Antoine and his mother met me at the airport in his hometown of Aix-en-Provence after I had spent nearly two months humping through Iraq at the height of the war. I had reported where I could, eaten where I could, and slept where I could—which included mud and stone huts and, if I was lucky, sodden cots in prefab barracks in godforsaken American forward operating bases, or FOBs. I was so hairy, dirty, and stinky as I exited the airport's baggage area that my son did not even recognize me until I showered and shaved. I think I scared him.

In the meanwhile, that summer I flew Liam-Antoine, his mother, and her boyfriend to the States so he could stay with me while they toured New England. The following summer, when he was four, he flew over with his aunt and uncle, whom I had invited to my home. (It was good to live near an ocean beach!) After the boy turned five, he regularly flew to the States by himself to spend not only the summers but also every fall, Christmas, and spring school vacation with me. He learned to "do" Halloween from his American cousins—the French do not celebrate the holiday—and for several years we made it a habit to visit Disney World either in February or April.

So despite the fact that Liam-Antoine is living his entire life in France with his mother, I still manage to see him at least three to four times a year. Yet in the same way I always tell myself upon Liam-Antoine's departures how quickly the time will fly before his next visit, it never does. Now I wondered if Terry felt the same about all of his "babies" to whom he grows so close only to have to hand them over to others.

"If you mean some kind of separation anxiety, well, I guess there's a little of that," he said with a slight shrug. "I suppose I've felt that way about every single dog we've placed. Some more strongly than others. But let's face it, that's the business we're in. Plus, in the end, there are very few of these dogs that I will *never* see again."

I'm not certain I bought his explanation, but it was his story and he was sticking to it.

Once we were across the river, Lakin was but a few miles down a rural two-lane blacktop that wound into rural West Columbia, a patchwork of farm fields and wild woods. The low winter sky was the color of brushed aluminum as we pulled into the visitor's parking area and were met by Phil Putney, a former corrections officer who is now a corrections counselor at Lakin. The promotion makes Phil paws4prisons' "point man" at the facility. A stout, genial thirty-five-year-old with an easy gait and a mustache as thick as a fruit bat, Phil grabbed Terry in a bear hug before shaking my hand. He then stooped to learn the names of each puppy before leading us through the institution's double-reinforced entrance door.

Lakin is West Virginia's only all-female state prison—the female-only Alderson is a federal prison—housing around 450 inmates who range from minimum- to maximum-security status. The state's Department of Corrections had certified the paws4prisons program two years earlier, and Phil told me that only nonviolent inmates below a certain "threat level" are allowed to apply to be trainers. The most difficult part of his job, he added, has been differentiating between inmates who volunteered because they really wanted to throw their all into working with the dogs and those who saw the project as an easy out from general population work details.

"Those kind don't do me any good, they don't do Terry any good, they don't do the dogs any good," he said with a syrupy twang. "You just do your best to weed them out. Little easier now that I've been on the job for a while. Funny thing is, there's really no correlation between the crimes they're in for and their abilities as dog handlers. I've seen some of the worst offenders make the best trainers, and vice versa."

After showing identification, depositing my wallet and loose change into a lobby strongbox, and signing a government waiver forbidding me from identifying any prisoner by name, I passed through the metal detector next to the admitting desk with Terry and Phil. A buzzer sounded, and a set of thick steel inner doors opened. They slammed shut behind us as Phil led Terry, me, and the leashed dogs into an empty visitation room lined with rows of metal folding chairs. A moment later, nine female inmates ranging in age from twenty to fifty-five filed in. The prisoners were black, white, Asian, American Indian. In another life they had been drug dealers, check kiters, bail jumpers, and, here at Lakin, one murderer. They wore baggy khaki jumpsuits and red vests embroidered with the initials "p4p."

As usual, for weeks prior to our arrival, Phil had been in e-mail contact with Terry, Kyria, and CeCe Miller, the director of Assistance Dog Training programs at paws4prisons. (CC, like David Burry, is another former Hazelton inmate whom Terry brought into the p4p fold after her release.) Phil had gleaned as much information as possible about each pup's personality. He had then pre-assigned each inmate a dog, hoping to complement the animal's temperament with its handler's.

Sometimes, Phil told me, opposites attract, and it works best to place a shy dog with a brash, outgoing trainer. At other times, usually at Terry and Kyria's suggestion, he will counterintuitively select, say, a particularly intelligent handler or a particularly hard-headed handler to work with a dog that exhibits similar traits. Either way, he admitted, at such an early stage in the process, this was all more educated guesswork than science, and it was not unusual for Phil to observe a trainer spending a few days with a dog before switching the animal to another inmate.

Meanwhile, it was obvious that these women were anxious to meet their new charges. I wasn't sure what to expect, but I didn't expect this: These allegedly hardened criminals cooed and burbled while they embraced and petted the dogs—much the same reaction I had observed in Kyria's young students. As Terry introduced each pup to its new handlers—a primary and an assistant—it seemed that I was the only one thinking about those steel doors that had closed behind us. The sound evoked the memory of David Burry's words about the prison gate slamming shut behind him: "You're on the threshold of a new life, leaving the old one behind. You can choose a path—to change for the good or to feel sorry for yourself and stew in this immense bitterness."

I glanced about the room. I sensed little stewing. In fact, the inmates could barely suppress their excitement. It was as if Terry, Phil, and I were not even present, and we stood off to the side for a moment to allow another short round of cuddling and caressing before Terry finally asked for quiet. The inmates took seats in a semicircle around him, their leashed trainees at their feet. Terry cleared his throat, ran his hand through Chaeney's scruff, and began to speak.

For all his fear of public speaking, Terry does a surprisingly good job of it when he has to. He does not hem or pace or even interject his sentences with time-buying nervous tics, such as "er" or "you know."

Standing tall before the inmates, meeting their eyes, he began with the basics in a clear, strong voice. He bent over, placed one of his hands under a dog's rump, and lifted it high before him. "This is how you always—always—pick them up," he said. "They're still young enough to carry like this."

Then he grabbed the dog by the scruff on the back of its neck. "Never like this," he said.

Next he threw the dog over his shoulder. "Never like this."

Then he balanced the pup's four paws in the palm of his hand. "And never, ever, ever like this."

The room broke up, even Phil cracked a smile, and with the laughter I could sense Terry's mood lightening. Once again it struck me that though Terry may be uncomfortable addressing a roomful of people, with a dog in his arms he becomes a different person.

He told the inmates that aside from treats for tasks well done, they were only to feed the puppies at the prescribed meal times, once in the morning and once at night. Anyone caught breaking this rule would be expelled from the program. The inmates all nodded. Then he explained that certain restrictions—no humping, no playful biting ("No mouth, no!")—had been reinforced since the dogs were three days old, and he stressed that from here on in there was also to be no group play.

"They are here for business, not fun," he said. He then warned his audience that the first two or three days were going to be the most difficult as the dogs acclimated to their new surroundings.

The puppies had lived together in the small confines of the Wilmington center's kennel room since their births, and because of this, he told the handlers, nighttime in particular was going to be hard on them in the beginning. For the first time they would not be sleeping in a pile with one another—rather, each pup would be alone in a cell in a plastic carry-kennel at the foot of its assigned inmate's bunk. Under no circumstances, he warned, were they to be let out of their kennels.

"Some of you have trained dogs for me before," he said. "You know from experience that they will cry for each other's company in the beginning. I have no doubt this will break your hearts. But you have to learn to ignore it. Trust me, they will get used to their new home here."

At this, I noticed that a few of the pups—including the male I had dubbed the "shy one" back in the motel parking lot and the smallish female with the white blaze—were straining at their leashes to be closer to one another. Their handlers gently pulled them apart.

Then Terry's voice turned flinty as he expounded on the p4p philosophy and told the women what he expected from them.

"You will certainly come to like these dogs," he said. "You will probably come to love these dogs. But never forget, this is a business. You have been selected for this program because of your ability to train these dogs. If I find that you cannot train these dogs, if I find that you are treating these dogs as pets, I will fire you from the program. Are there any questions?"

The room was silent. I was reminded of the day I met Terry, the hard man seated at the center of a circle of wounded warriors at Fort Stewart.

Finally, several corrections officers entered the visitation room to escort us through the corridors of the institution's main building. We passed inmates from the general population whose hands flicked to sneak brisk pets when the officers weren't looking, and we passed others who merely scowled. When we paused before the entrance to the mess hall, Terry reiterated that each handler was to train her dog to lie quietly under the table during communal meals. If anyone was caught sneaking scraps to a dog, she would be expelled from the program. Some of the inmates nodded, others side-eyed the dogs, perhaps afraid to meet Terry's stone face.

All the while it was evident that the young dogs were confused by the alien assaults on their senses, by the fluorescent light tubes flickering overhead, by the clang of cell doors slamming shut, by the distinctive and pervasive odor—a sort of disinfectant-meets-perspiration—peculiar to prisons and jails everywhere. But most of all, the dogs were spooked by the presence of so many strangers. Whenever possible, they attempted to close ranks, huddling together like a flock of frightened sheep. They appeared emotionally drained by the time we reached Lakin's "Dog Wing," where awaiting us in the dayroom were another two dozen paws4prisons handlers and nearly as many dogs in various stages of training. They were all Goldens or Labs.

Now Terry dropped his stern facade and greeted each animal by name. There was a sort of controlled pandemonium as the twenty or so dogs—newcomers and old timers who ranged from eleven months to two years old—mingled and sniffed and yipped and barked. Our plan had been to deliver the puppies, meet their handlers, say a quick hello to the rest of the prisoners in the program, and hit the road for the three-hour drive to Alderson. But as a kind of gift to the inmates, in recognition of their hard work and good behavior, Phil Putney had organized a presentation in Terry's honor.

So Terry and I settled onto a well-worn leather couch braced against an institutional-gray concrete wall while a succession of two-women handling teams strode to the center of the room, introduced themselves and their dog, and gave a brief demonstration of how far its training had progressed. The commands were for the most part fairly simple and repetitive. Each team was satisfied to demonstrate their dog's mastery of "stay" and "sit," of "speak" and "heel."

Perhaps three-quarters of the animals obeyed well, their handlers self-evidently proud of their progress. Half of the remainder eventually performed their tasks after much cajoling. The rest were, well, lacking. One Golden Retriever had each task down pat; unfortunately, he heeled when he was ordered to sit and spoke when he was ordered to stay. His handlers turned beet red. Another, a black Lab, was so hyper that he tore back and forth across the room for a good five minutes before his trainers could corner and leash him. After fifteen minutes or so of trying to get him to sit still, they gave up. They apologized to Terry and promised their dog would be tip-top next time.

Terry remained stone-silent, but I could literally feel him squirming on the couch cushion beside me. He hated being the center of so much attention—and, truth be told, I sensed that he was somewhat bored—but he never interrupted the program to offer advice or even to ask any team to speed it along. David Burry again crossed my mind. *Patience is the key.* As the exhibition stretched into its third hour, he leaned over and whispered, "Forget Alderson today. We'll come back first thing tomorrow morning and pick up the dogs for transfer." It was nearing dusk by the time we rose to leave.

I had spoken to several of the inmates during breaks. Despite Terry's standoffishness, they seemed genuinely awed to be in the presence of the executive director of paws4people. He was their rock star. One tough-looking woman introduced herself as Geneva and told me that the paws4prisons program had literally given her something to live for.

Geneva sported a blonde buzz cut and biceps the size and texture of large walnuts. Her eyes were green and her voice was a rasp, like an adze being scraped over a hardwood board. She had, she said, been sentenced two decades earlier to "life plus ten" for running down a young boy while drunk. The child died. She was so high she did not even remember the accident when she sobered up. But, she said, the boy's death had haunted her close to madness. During her first few years in Lakin, she acquired a reputation as a troublemaker and was busted several times for fighting with both other inmates and corrections officers. She was also caught in possession of smuggled drugs, alcohol, and cigarettes.

"When I first got here, I was mean and angry, an out-of-control addict; a terrible person who made a terrible mistake," she said. "I would not recognize that person today. I've been with the dog program a couple years now, and I know I'm never leaving this place. But these dogs, and the thought of what they do once *they* get out, are one of the few things that keep me going."

Phil had told me earlier that even the women with the wildest reputations in the general population seemed to undergo a personality change once they were accepted into the paws4prisons program.

"Even the ones who know they're never making parole. They don't want to screw up down here and return to the general population. There's a long line to get into this program, and we don't give many second chances."

The success of that day's exhibitions seemed proof. Of course, it didn't hurt that p4p trainers also enjoyed certain perks aside from the canine companionship—bigger cells with private bathrooms, for instance—not granted to the facility's general population.

As we bid our goodbyes, a petite brunette tapped me on the shoulder. I noticed that she had waited to approach me until Terry turned his back to converse with Phil, like she was afraid of getting too near him. When she saw her chance, she scooted toward me tilting forward with stooped shoulders, as if she were toting a rucksack full of rocks.

I guessed she was in her midtwenties. Delicate acne scars etched the corners of her mouth.

She said she'd been sentenced for selling amphetamines. Her voice fell midway between a whisper and a squeak. "You know the marines?" she asked.

When we'd first entered the Dog Wing, Terry had briefly introduced me as a visiting journalist whose specialty was covering the military. Now this mousy woman said she wanted to show me something. She pulled a creased photograph from her jumpsuit pocket and handed it to me. It was a picture of a big-eyed, handsome kid. He was wearing his dress blues, the formal marine corps uniform.

"My baby brother," she said. She told me he had survived

multiple deployments to Iraq and Afghanistan. I mentioned I had been to both countries on assignment. She began to weep.

"He's dead now," she said. *Jesus.* He looked so young in that photo, not much older than Liam-Antoine. I suppose I must have said, "How?" although I don't remember uttering a word.

"He crashed his Harley Davidson on a Florida highway a couple of months ago," she said. "It's the reason I joined this program. If I can help train a Service Dog that goes to a veteran who needs help . . . "

She began to cry harder, deep silent breaths convulsing her shoulders, and she could not finish her sentence. I instinctively reached out to put an arm around her but pulled it back before I made contact with her shoulders. Other than a handshake, I did not know if I was allowed to touch the inmates.

Her weeping caught Terry's attention, and he turned and raised an eyebrow. He took a half-step toward us and stopped. I sensed that he wanted to comfort her, but I also suspected he did not know how. A split second later, a dozen or so inmates gathered around the weeping little brunette like football players in a huddle. As Phil escorted us out of the Dog Wing and through the long corridor leading to the front lobby, I looked back over my shoulder. Her fellow inmates were still consoling the woman who had missed her brother's funeral because she was behind bars for selling amphetamines.

Later, at the motel, I told Terry the story. He shook his head sadly and wondered if the marine's death had truly been an accident.

"I wonder how many of these fatal *accidents* by combat vets are really PTSD-induced suicides?" he said. "More of them than we'll ever know, I suspect."

"Get a good night's sleep," he said with a weary smile. "Lotta traveling tomorrow."

Chapter Five

The Slammer (2)

"C'mon! Stimulate!"

Kyria shoots her dad a look. *Duh.* As if she wasn't already trying her best to awaken the latest arrival.

Puppy number five joins our world at 3:01 a.m. Off-white and burly, he—yes, another boy—does not stir as Terry slits the sac, severs and clips the umbilical cord, and hands him to Kyria. I stand there helplessly with my piece of white yarn as Kyria gives the newborn a full-body massage and Claire licks and licks, but it is still a good thirty seconds (that feel more like minutes) before the pup, soon to be named Myer, twitches his limbs and begins to mewl. When they place him on the scale, he ties Lawson for weightiest yet at just over a pound and a half.

Meanwhile, Kyria's students remain enthralled by the sight of the newborns. David is playing it cool, but Savannah and Mallory "ooh" and "aww" each time one of the puppies does something "cute." Which is to say, each time one or another does *anything.*

In truth, the cuteness factor in the whelping room is off the charts, and I am not surprised at the kids' reactions. Studies by neuroscientists suggest that the snub noses, high foreheads, floppy ears, and large, wide-set eyes of newborn puppies excite the same circuitry in our brains that reacts to human babies. Humans evolved to protect newborns and toddlers until they can fend for themselves—the larger the clan, the safer the clan—and as a result of that complex evolutionary development, people are drawn not only to the physical appearance of human infants but also to the physical appearance of newborns of almost every mammalian species. Among those species, primates and dogs rank among the highest.

In fact, one of the reasons breeds such as Golden Retrievers and Labradors make such terrific Assistance Dogs is that they retain these infantile characteristics throughout their lives. The scientific name for this is *neotenization,* and it is evident in our attraction to big-eyed "baby faces," from pandas to ET phoning home to cartoon characters like Betty Boop and Mickey Mouse.

By keeping what is known as this infant schema for life—physically *and* emotionally—what dog trainers call droopy breeds (such as Golden Retrievers, Labradors, Newfoundlands, and even Saint Bernards) separate themselves from other dogs that become more "pointy" as they grow older. Think of mature Shepherds, Terriers, Dobermans, and Collies with their long snouts, peaked ears, and more outward-set eyes. As a general rule, the physical appearance of pointy dogs not only subconsciously sparks our prehistoric fear of predatory wolves, but studies have found that these physical characteristics also reflect a difference in temperament.

Researchers can only guess at the causes for this—breeding for certain tasks, such as hunting and herding, is a leading hypothesis. Nonetheless, multiple canine studies have determined that as dogs like German Shepherds and Collies age, they will begin to reason at a higher level than a neotenized breed. This could make for a wonderful guard dog or sheep herder, but it also leaves pointy dogs more difficult to train. A good 45 percent of German Shepherds flunk out of Seeing Eye programs, for instance. And like a teenager asked to do his chores (over and over and over), the ones who do matriculate respond more readily to the harsh discipline of an alpha owner as opposed to an owner who merely wants to coexist with his pet.

Conversely, dog experts liken even mature neotenized breeds to human toddlers in terms of emotional capacity. A Golden Retriever's or Labrador's intrinsic nature, like a small child's, is to please. They by and large adapt more willingly to a loving parental figure than to a steely disciplinarian. There are always exceptions, of course. Kyria's first Golden Retriever, Riley, comes to mind. But for the most part, the owner of a neotenized dog will get better results with honey than with vinegar.

"The dogs who keep their childlike features, who have that puppy thing going for their entire lives, give us a leg up on the training process," Terry says as we watch the college students fussing over the pups. "I think that's what got a lot of these kids into Kyria's classes in the first place. Most of them take the course as an elective; they're not going to be working with Assistance Dogs once they graduate. But what they've learned with her, with us, they'll take with them through their lives.

"They've met some of our clients now and seen how the dogs have changed lives. More than a few have admitted to us, 'Holy cow, I had no idea a dog could do that.' So what are they going to do twenty, thirty years from now because of their exposure to this? Will the companies that they'll be running be a little more friendly to people with disabilities? Will they be able to fund an organization like us because they know the dogs are helping kids in wheelchairs or combat veterans who were willing to sacrifice their lives or, yes, even prisoners trying to rehabilitate themselves?"

And here Terry reaches for Myer and gently lifts his ears.

"And it all starts with these floppy things," he says. "Nuts, huh?"

∙━━━━━━━━━━∙

The filmy winter sunlight had barely crested the towering Appalachians when Phil Putney led the three dogs bound for Alderson through Lakin's front gate. Findley and Sidney, twenty-month-old Golden Retrievers and sisters, were so sleek, elegant, and regal they appeared to prance instead of walk. Terry mentioned that p4p had acquired them from a certified breeder in Michigan whom he trusted implicitly. Their good bloodlines, combined with the fact that both had recently aced their eye, heart, and hip physicals, made them excellent potential breeders. The majority of p4p dogs are spayed or neutered at some point during the training process, but given Findley's and Sidney's pedigree and robust health, Terry and Kyria would likely mate them with similar males.

He was not as sanguine about Jarrett, a fourteen-month-old rescue dog. The silver and black Labrador mix had gone through several inmate handlers, but his training was just not taking. "Too neurotic" was Terry's diagnosis.

He wasn't certain of the cause of Jarrett's dysfunction. You never knew with rescue dogs. Perhaps he was beaten as a puppy or starved or abandoned. Or all three. In fact, Jarrett really had no business being transferred from Lakin without having yet mastered his rudimentary commands. But Terry had taken a liking to the recalcitrant Lab, and in this one case he was making an exception to p4p rules. He hoped that, like a ballplayer mired in a slump,

Who needs pillows when you have a fluffy Riley? Twelve-year-old Kyria Henry's first dog, Riley (shown here in 1999 acting as a backstop as Brielle receives a sweet neck rub), became the impetus for the creation of paws4people.

Even a year later, in 2000, Terry may still be wondering what his daughter talked him into as he shows his own Assistance Dog, Addie, all the love before they both head out to work with children in special needs classes.

Kyria Henry, holding a five-day-old Golden Retriever puppy. As with all newborn dogs, it will be a couple of weeks before this little guy opens his eyes and sees the world.

It wasn't all smiles when paws4vets client April Cooke and Claire undertook their Public Access training under the tutelage and watchful eye of paws4people board member David Burry. But as you can see, all's well that ends well.

April Cooke and Claire celebrate with big kisses after successfully completing their Public Access training.

Annie Moran takes a break from the annual paws4people 5-K run in Wilmington, North Carolina, to give a big hug to April Cooke's Service Dog, Claire.

After living with debilitating PTSD for more than three decades since his Vietnam service, US Army veteran Walter Parker says that his pairing with Jackson (who the author is proud to have helped birth) has changed his life.

Emilia Bartlinski says the best part about having Mayzie at her side was that the night before her numerous surgeries to correct her crippling osteomyelitis, Mayzie jumped up into her bed and snuggled with her. An added bonus: Emilia's doctors made special provisions to permit Mayzie to enter the operating and recovery rooms wearing a custom-made hospital gown.

Drake, a paws4vets Service Dog, checks out the competition as he awaits his turn to perform at the rally competition held every year at the paws4people family reunion.

There's just something about paws4vets that draws an inordinate amount of US Marine Corps veterans to the program. Here, former leatherneck Roger Dudley takes a load off with his new best friend, Ashe. We're guessing the sly smiles give away their love for each other.

Somber black Lab Solomon Bumped with Erin Buckles after she was surgically separated from her conjoined twin, Jade, and suffered severe complications.

"Before Solomon, Erin was so inhibited," says Erin's mom, Melissa. "She was the kid in the wheelchair all the other kids stared at. Now, she's the girl with the cool dog. She even joined a power wheelchair soccer league. God chooses all our paths."

Despite her skittish performance in front of the author at her first Bump, pretty Golden Retriever Avery has come a long way, including acquiring the discipline to balance a treat on her nose until her new partner, US Navy veteran Robbie Combs, gives her the signal to go ahead and gobble away.

Josh Gregor and his Medical Alert Service Dog, Mason, are inseparable. Josh was born with a genetic syndrome that allows him to eat only through a tube inserted into his abdomen. "Sometimes, especially at night, that tube gets crinkled up and clogged," says Josh's mom, Tracey. "Mason lets us know right away. More importantly, Josh just needed a best buddy. Now he has one."

"If you just want to sit at home and die, that's your right," says Vietnam veteran and paws4vets client Sonny Morrow, shown here in his wheelchair with his Assistance Dog, Jake. "I didn't want that to happen to me. Jake made sure it didn't."

Since Bumping with her Service Dog, Dawson, 28-year-old graphic designer Rachael Wessell has been a "hell on wheels" fundraiser for paws4people. "I suppose technically I have cerebral palsy," she says with an impish grin. "But that's not how I look at my world. I just consider myself someone who gets around differently."

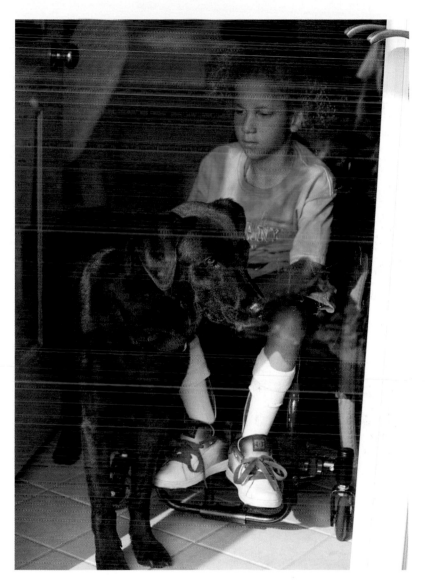

Erin Buckles and Solomon may be getting older—and more contemplative—each time we turn the page. Nonetheless, she still knows how to style with her white kicks and pink laces.

Alex Crisp, shown here with his parents, Matt and Kathy, was one of paws4people's first client recipients. His Mobility Service Dog, Camden, helps Alex—whose mitochondrial disease limits his movement—with everything from his physical therapy to his medical procedures to his schoolwork. No wonder Alex's smile is off the charts.

When former marine Tony Mullis lost both his legs to an IED blast in Afghanistan, he wondered if he would ever be able to enjoy his favorite hobbies of hunting and fishing again. He sure did, once he Bumped with his chocolate Lab Service Dog, Madison. "In the marines, there is always someone there to watch your back," Tony says. "That is what I am here to do for my wife and son. Now I have a friend who can do the same for me."

Alex Keefover—with a gleeful assist from his mom, Jennifer—takes time off from his mathematics studies at West Virginia's Fairmont State University to show off Kingsley's skills in the rally competition held every year at the paws4people family reunion.

Where would paws4people be without its indefatigable community outreach coordinator, Renee Johnson, and her Service Dog, Travis? Renee, a navy veteran, has become the de facto major domo at the organization's Wilmington headquarters, volunteering for jobs ranging from filling out paperwork to ordering dog blankets to cleaning up after messy births.

When former marine 1st lieutenant and Purple Heart recipient Will Reiser graduated from the United States Naval Academy and shipped out for his multiple deployments to Afghanistan, he probably never expected that Golden Retriever Morgan would become his best friend and constant companion, helping him cope with his traumatic brain injury. But, as they say, good things come in furry packages.

Kyria Henry doesn't travel anywhere without her Service Dog Ambassador, Wyatt, a gorgeous black Lab who has full public access to the many events, speaking engagements, and fundraisers Kyria attends. "Wyatt represents everything all our Service Dogs can do," says Kyria.

Looks like someone snapped the notoriously camera-shy Terry Henry when he wasn't looking. Terry realizes that all eyes will be on beautiful Service Dogs, left to right, Chaeney, Travis, and Bradie Lynn.

Natalie Kiddie utilizes her Service Dog, Dolce, while counseling children in a facility for juveniles in northern Virginia. Many paws4people dogs who are not placed with clients are trained to work with mental health professionals like Natalie, who have their dogs certified by p4p as Facility Dogs.

a change of scenery might spark a transformation in Jarrett. The imperturbable Chaeney stretched and yawned as the three new-comers, their frozen breath condensing into puffs of fog, settled in beside him in the bed of the old Saturn. With luck we'd make Alderson sometime in late morning.

By 9:00 we were halfway across the state. The jagged granite mountain peaks, snow-dusted and stark, were both beautiful and oddly menacing. My ears popped as Terry raced at seventy miles per hour up one side of a mountain and down the other into West Virginia's famous gorges and hollers. Every so often we would spot a spire of dove-gray smoke rising from what appeared an impenetrable dell deep in the woods. When I made a crack about moonshiners and revenue men, Terry's response was a sly smile.

"You think you're joking," he said. "But you ain't."

Terry liked driving. I wondered what book on tape he would be listening to if I weren't along for the ride and yammering in his ear. His many trips along these roads had left him with a knowl-edge of the terrain, and he frequently pointed out mountains where Civil War armies had marched to and fro and rivers that, in the spring he said, provide some of the best whitewater rafting east of the Missouri.

Around 10:00 we stopped at a roadside diner where, Terry said, the homemade scones were some of the best he'd ever tasted. We both ordered the raspberry with our coffees, and the conversation turned to yesterday's visit to Lakin. I had never given much thought to prisons and prisoners before. Oh, I had a vague notion that our nation's incarceration rate is a disgrace for a First World country, as is the percentage of America's black pop-ulation behind bars. I also had a shallow awareness of the physical and psychological deprivations inmates face from both guards and fellow prisoners. But spending the day with the ladies of Lakin had given me a perspective on human nature that surprised me. It was almost as if, while those inmates were training the dogs, the dogs were in turn training them—helping them to rehabilitate from their broken pasts, from their former lives as drug dealers and drunk drivers who ran over children.

"You've heard of win-win?" I said to Terry. "Well, I see your prison project as a win-win-win. For the inmates. For the dogs, particularly the rescue dogs like Jarrett. And for the clients with whom the dogs are ultimately placed."

He smiled. "I'll add a fourth win to that," he said. "For every one of us associated with the process. The universe—God—has allowed me the opportunity to do what I'm doing. I could still be driving a truck. I could still be back in 1995 suckin' on pain pills and hidin' in corners."

Back in the Saturn after walking the dogs, Terry set the Alderson scene for me. "No fences there," he said, "so the dogs can start learning to deal with distractions like squirrels and birds. And the inmate population is much more integrated with the staff, specifically the male corrections officers, so the dogs become more accustomed to being around men. By the time they reach the next stage, Hazelton or Prunytown, they're ready to develop even more skill sets. Once a week the inmates at those camps are allowed to take the dogs on day trips. Visit malls, cross busy streets, mingle in crowds."

He reminded me that for the first year or so of the animals' lives—from birth right up through their stay at Lakin—they rarely encountered such stimuli. "It's really kind of neat to watch the learning process unfold," he said. "You only caught a little of that yesterday."

We pulled off the interstate and began a steep climb up a narrow switchback road. Far below, an ice-crusted river flanked our right. To our left, a sheer wall of rocky earth loomed like a battlement pocked with copses of beech, red maple, birch, and mixed oak. At the top of the rise, the road wound into a clearing, and then past an unmanned gate. It was open, and we drove through it onto the grounds of the Alderson Federal Prison Camp.

Christened in 1927, Alderson is the oldest female prison in the United States. If its name rings a bell, it may be because the facility has hosted inmates as diverse as the chanteuse Billie Holiday, who served a ten-month stint there in the late 1940s for possession of narcotics, to the deranged Manson acolyte Lynette "Squeaky" Fromme, who spent the majority of her thirty-four-year sentence in Alderson after her failed assassination attempt on President Gerald Ford. Martha Stewart is also an alumna. She served five months in 2005 for obstruction of justice.

The Alderson complex is spread over 160 wooded acres in the southeast corner of the state, and if, as Terry suggested, I should try to imagine it as the equivalent of a paws4prisons' high school, it was one of the fanciest I had ever seen. With its leafy bridle paths, volleyball courts, and two-story Georgian-style dormitories fronted by ionic columns and filigreed balconies, it looked less like "The Slammer" and more like a New England boarding school—after which, as a matter of fact, it had been modeled. The commons section is still referred to as the campus, and during Martha Stewart's stay, the press had dubbed it "Camp Cupcake."

Inside the administration building, Terry introduced me to Terri Martin, a tall woman whose long, blonde, jouncing curls fell past the shoulders of her pinstriped business suit. Terri Martin, Alderson's longtime "education specialist," also ran the facility's paws4prisons project, the counterpart to Lakin's Phil Putney. We underwent the usual security protocols before the three of us traipsed across a manicured greensward bisected by gravel paths with the leashed Findley, Sidney, and Jarrett. At the far end of the quadrangle, we entered the dormitory that housed Terri Martin's office and an adjacent dayroom.

Once inside, she explained that the federal prison system recognizes projects such as paws4prisons as "vocational programs," along the lines of GED-equivalency classes and cosmetology courses. Moreover, unlike at the state-run Lakin, inmates applying to become p4p trainers at Alderson must be high school graduates or have earned their GED certificates. Once accepted into the program, they can accumulate sixteen college credits for every five hundred hours of work. She said that forty-eight dogs had passed through the Alderson program, and several p4p handlers had been paroled or released as state-certified dog trainers.

While Terry Henry settled Findley, Sidney, and Jarrett into carry-kennels, I explored what was obviously the seat of Alderson's canine operation. Makeshift bookshelves bulged with dog-care manuals and instructional titles—*The Power of Positive Dog Training, Don't Shoot the Dog!, Puppies for Dummies, How to Teach a New Dog Old Tricks*. A whiteboard on one wall maintained schedules for upcoming p4p events—Command Training, Open Training, Dogs at Field—Play & Exercise—while another listed dates and times for written examinations on subjects ranging from Canine Reproduction to Immunology/First Aid. My favorite touch was the announcement for the Car Loading and Unloading Clinic. How difficult could it be to get a dog in and out of a vehicle?

Terri Martin had inaugurated the p4p program three years earlier, but I sensed a more formal business relationship between her and Terry Henry than he had with Phil Putney. Terri Martin had arranged to spend the day conducting a series of interviews with a half-dozen inmates recently accepted into the program as entry-level trainers—she had vetted them, and now it was up to Terry Henry to give them his stamp of approval. But first the prison's lead trainer, a husky brunette serving five years for drug crimes, stopped by. Terry Henry had promoted her a few months earlier after her predecessor was paroled, and he greeted her with a formal handshake and introduced her to the new dogs.

The lead trainer scooted down on all fours and made the usual fuss over each of the animals while Terry Henry gave her a brief status report on the dogs, including the fact that Jarrett might have some kind of learning disability that prevented him from processing and following commands.

"See what you think after you've had him a few days," Terry Henry said. "I kind of have a soft spot for that dog, but if he can't cut it . . . well, I'm anxious to see if you can do anything with him."

The lead trainer gave Jarrett a last pet, rose, and before exiting handed Terry a sheath of progress reports on the half-dozen dogs already training in the complex. The interviews were scheduled next, but before we all took seats at a long table, Terri Martin mentioned that there was something else to sort out.

"It's, um, about some of the inmates," she said. "Some trouble with them, actually."

Despite her wan smile, it was obvious she was nervous reporting to Terry whatever this "trouble" was. She paced the room, sat down, got up, paced a few steps more, and finally got to it. Lately, she said, petty rivalries had arisen among the dog handlers, leading to frequent arguments. As a result, she went on, the inmates had divided into cliques and morale was plummeting. It was affecting everyone's work.

Terry nodded for her to go on. I could not read his stony face. I knew he liked and respected Terri Martin; he had told me as much on several occasions.

Terri Martin said the focus of the bad blood was the program's new lead trainer, whom several of the handlers had accused of showing favoritism to her friends when assigning tasks and schedules. There had been sulking and pouting, she said, and even a few shouting matches.

From a prison administrator's point of view, this was the worst turn of events short of outright violence. In theory, every inmate serving time in America's state and federal prisons—yes, even p4p lead trainers—must by law be considered, and treated as, equals. Technically, no one is allowed to "give orders." Of course, in actuality this is not how incarceration works at any level in this country or, for that matter, anywhere else on the planet. Some people, for myriad reasons, are just better equipped to lead, and in worst-case scenarios the strong will always prey on the weak. But for this dynamic to have bled into Alderson's p4p program was distressing.

Terry Henry interrupted her with a wave of his hand. "I really have no patience for this," he said. She nodded.

"Bottom line," he continued, "I like the lead trainer. She's good with my dogs. They come out of here knowing what to do. If some of the other handlers don't like her, we'll just have to get rid of them and find new ones."

This was followed by what I took as a nod to diplomacy. "I completely understand that you're in charge in here, Terri," he said. "But, my suggestion? Fire the malcontents."

It sure did not sound like a "suggestion" to me. But Terri Martin nodded again. She looked a little shaken. I wondered what she expected. She had been working with Terry Henry for years, surely long enough to recognize how rigid he could be about always—always—putting the well-being of his animals ahead of their faceless trainers. Perhaps paws4people clients were a different story. I had been around the organization long enough to see Terry weep when he told stories of the disabled kids with whom he had worked and with whom p4p had placed dogs, to watch him truly and emotionally commiserate with their parents over their plights, to refuse to give up on veterans like Jeff Mitchell. But those clients had earned Terry's trust. As had, apparently, Alderson's head trainer.

It seemed to me that, once again, Terry Henry was refusing to let anyone inside his thick emotional shell who had not earned it. The former inmates David Burry and CeCe Miller now working for p4p? They had earned it. It had taken some time, but they had burrowed their way through. But the squabbling prisoners at Alderson? Not yet, not yet by a long shot. Didn't Terri Martin get this?

"Should we begin the interviews?" she said.

Terry Henry shook his head.

<hr />

The half-dozen new entry-level trainers had never before met Terry Henry, but his hard-ass reputation preceded him. They had been working in the paws4prisons program on a kind of probationary basis, and they were aware that this was probably their only chance to convince him that they were worthy to remain full time. To that end, what followed resembled not so much job interviews as much as pieces of performance art.

Like some kind of courtroom scene, Terry Henry, Terri Martin, and I settled in behind a long table facing a lone chair in the middle of the room. The prison official, pen poised, withdrew a legal pad from her briefcase. Terry Henry took no notes as the lead trainer escorted the inmates in one at a time. As at Lakin, the women were all ages, shapes, and sizes; black, brown, and white.

With each inmate, Terry Henry began with the same statement: "Tell me about yourself and why you want to work with my dogs."

One short, beefy woman, serving seventy-eight months for credit card fraud, said the paws4prisons program had provided her with "a sense of accomplishment, pride, and self-esteem" that she'd never felt on the outside. Another, whose face resembled a welder's mask and who had been convicted of selling crystal meth, promised that when she got out, she would devote the rest of her life to working with rescue dogs.

The women were all nervous, but they displayed those nerves in different manners. Some approached the chair as if there might be snakes under it, and a few punctuated their answers with girly-girl giggles. One inmate in particular either would not, or could not, stop talking. She was a brassy, plump blonde, somewhere in her early thirties, and she spoke with a pronounced drawl. She told us she had been arrested and convicted in Virginia a year earlier for drug conspiracy after her boyfriend died in a car accident and she'd taken over his marijuana, meth, and cocaine "dealership." She said the word as if she had sold used Hondas.

"I know it was wrong, but I didn't know what else to do," she said. "I'd never really worked a real job in my life, and the money was good, and it seemed so easy, and the lifestyle was fun, and I rarely used my own product . . . "

On and on she rambled, giving us a detailed, inside look at the world of buying drugs wholesale from Mexican middlemen, how to cut them and where to store them (behind false garage walls), where the best retail opportunities arose (malls and college campuses), and how to recruit a student sales force (free samples). After fifteen minutes she was still regaling us with the inside dope, as it were, on the middle-class drug trade, and Terri Martin was increasingly side-eyeing Terry Henry, wondering how much more of this narrative he would sit through. After a few more minutes, he finally raised his hand to signal "enough." I had to stifle a laugh when the inmate ignored him and proceeded to offer a detailed explanation of the gradient levels of THC contained in different species of pot.

"Excuse me, excuse me, excuse me," Terry Henry finally interjected. "Would you mind moving on to why you want to work with my dogs?"

Incredibly, the prisoner smiled, nodded, and went right back to talking about the drug trade. Terry rolled his eyes, but to my surprise he let her continue. During a description of how many bags of marijuana constituted "felony weight," he grabbed my notebook and pen from my lap, scribbled "!?!?" onto a page, and handed it back to me.

The tiniest of smiles lifted the corners of his mouth. He was getting a kick out of this.

"But I've sure learned my lessons now," she concluded in her tidewater twang. "Ah'll never do it again, 'specially as long as this dog program can teach me to lairn a ways to make some money on the legal side when I get out."

She had, she said, shown that she had the knack to be a good businesswoman—aside, of course, from the getting-busted part—and she wanted to transfer those skills to the Service Dog industry upon her release.

After she'd stood, shaken our hands, paused to greet the new dogs, and left the room, Terry leaned toward me and said, "Sometimes it takes 'em a while to get there."

Again David Burry's credo crossed my mind: *Patience.* It worked with humans as well as dogs.

And we needed it, as the session lasted for the better part of the day. Every woman expressed contriteness over her crimes, and some shed tears as they told stories of the children, husbands, and parents they had let down. Before departing, each inmate inevitably stooped to play with Findley, Sidney, and Jarrett. This didn't strike me as a ploy. Scientific studies suggest that the lonelier the human, the more she will anthropomorphize a dog. Here, I supposed, was proof positive, as the inmates invariably addressed them in the usual baby-talk cadences.

One inmate with a memorable story was a mousy Hispanic girl, perhaps in her midtwenties, who was also serving nearly six years for selling drugs. She told us that she had gotten mixed up in the trade after her husband's infantry unit had been deployed to Iraq. She was lonely and frightened for him, she said, and her brother, a dealer, suggested she could make some quick cash to supplement his combat pay by acting as a delivery girl. She planned to stop selling drugs upon her husband's return from overseas, she said, but after his second tour of duty he was diagnosed with PTSD, and she felt lost and confused by his mood swings. Her dealer brother was her only comfort.

With this, Terry sat up a bit straighter. "Did your husband get help?" he asked. "Does he still get help for his condition?"

The woman said that he was enrolled in a program with the Department of Veterans Affairs—she was a little hazy on the particulars—and added that one of the reasons she wanted to be a part of paws4prisons was that she had depended on men her entire life—her father, her brother, her husband—and now it was her turn to stand up and take care of him.

"I've been a failure my whole life," she said, and her lower lip quivered. "Not now. I believe I am young enough to turn my life around, and that I have the strength of will to turn things around and make a better life for my family. I am asking you from the bottom of my heart to allow me to remain in this program."

Terry merely nodded and wished her good luck. Afterward, when the room was cleared, he asked for my thoughts. I told him that their stories all moved me, particularly the woman with the sick veteran husband. No matter their emotional and physical tics, I asked, wasn't it obvious that they were all trying to change things for the better?

He rolled his eyes at me. "You've been spending too much time with David Burry."

Then he turned to Terri Martin. "Good job," he said. "Most of them were okay. I felt a couple were just trying to get over on us. I'll call you next week."

On the drive back down the mountain he shot me the fish-eye. Then he softened.

"Three, four years ago, some of those stories would have choked me up, too," he said. "But you gotta remember, these gals are in prison for a reason. Some of them might turn it around. Others won't. I hope they all do, but I know that won't happen. So first and foremost my main concern is my dogs, how they're treated, how they're trained."

Which reminded me—as much as I had hoped that this week's "prison run" would give me a feel for the inmates working with p4p, I had also hoped to see some more, well, *dog* action.

"Don't worry about that," Terry said. "We'll be getting more than enough tomorrow at Hazelton."

He was not kidding.

<hr/>

Now *this* was prison. Imposing twenty-foot walls. Correction officers peering down from looming guard towers. Sullen inmates following our every movement from the corner of their hard eyes.

Morgan Freeman and Tim Robbins would feel at home. I could only imagine how intimidating the men's wing might be.

We had again first stopped by Lakin to pick up dogs ready for transfer—in this case, a chocolate Labrador (Madison) and three Golden Retrievers (Airley, Carson, and Willow). Again, Chaeney barely acknowledged the dogs as they scampered into the back of the SUV. We'd made Hazelton by noon, pulling up to the mountaintop complex's secure female facility, home to some six hundred felons whose crimes ranged from murder to counterfeiting to the ubiquitous drug dealing.

Terry pointed out the adjacent penitentiary for men with its electric fence and, in the distance, the scattered buildings that constituted the minimum-security camp where David Burry had been incarcerated. The dogs here at Hazelton, he said, rotated between indoor training with the female inmates and outdoor pre-Public Access courses with the male handlers.

The aptly named Lisa Christmas was paws4prisons' administrator on site. Lisa was a jolly woman who had overseen Terry and Kyria's flagship program since its inception, and she wore her smile like a badge. Lisa was a Bureau of Prisons vocation specialist in charge of the program's sixteen inmates and dozen or so dogs. She escorted us and the new dogs through several security checks until we reached the main prison building, which housed an open public area where the general population mingled.

The walls enclosing the huge space rose three stories; each floor was lined with two-bunk cells. The main room itself was pocked with tables to play cards or read, and the space hummed with a steady noise from television sets and running washing machines and dryers punctuated with grunts from prisoners working out in the weight-lifting stations. It smelled like the inside of a Clorox bottle.

Lisa ran an efficient ship. Every trainer, she said, was required to work with the dogs a minimum of one hour per day, four days per week. In reality it was usually more. She showed me a sheet listing 130 commands. The dogs, she said, needed to master four commands per week. As at Alderson, all potential trainers had to have earned a high school diploma or a GED equivalent. Lisa had also instituted a policy of not accepting, "with the rare exception," any applicants sentenced to less than two years, as it took nearly that much time to master the academic and medical aspects of the program, which included being conversant in everything from canine vaccinations to deworming.

We talked as we walked, our destination a large cell that served as the facility's paws4prisons headquarters. Gathered inside, lining the walls and awaiting us, was a complement of women—"the sisterhood," they called themselves—and they were dressed in the same khaki jumpsuits as at the other institutions, only here they had also added loose yellow smocks to the ensemble, like a highway road crew's vests, to designate themselves as p4p trainers. Lisa mentioned that entry-level trainers, or ELTs, spent about a year working with the dogs before they either mustered out of the program or were promoted to trainers.

Terry greeted the head trainer with a handshake and made sure his back was facing a corner of the room. I had traveled with him enough by now to recognize how uncomfortable he was being the center of attention, and I was probably the only person present who noticed him reflexively reach for Chaeney and run his hand through the dog's scruff. The head trainer was a tall, skinny blonde who was serving seventy-two months for dealing methamphetamine, and as in the other prisons, she dove right into her personal story.

She grew up in Montana, she said, and was not only physically abused by her police officer stepfather but also raped at the age of nine by a neighbor. At thirteen she ran away from home and was arrested a year later for possessing the drug ecstasy. As part of her plea bargain, she was shipped off to a Christian boarding school in Nebraska, and upon her release from the school two years later, she traveled to Las Vegas and found her biological father, who promptly put her to work as a drug courier crisscrossing the country. "The Greyhound System," she called it. Addicted to meth, she was arrested twelve times in several states. Finally, two years ago, she was nabbed in New Jersey holding three ounces of the drug. Next stop, Hazelton.

She ran through her life's low points in a matter-of-fact manner, as if she were describing someone else, and I found myself admiring her forthrightness. She shed no tears while recounting her rough childhood—it was what it was—and I suspected from her delivery that she had come to terms not only with her scary upbringing but also with her mistakes.

Terry had told me beforehand that she had already inquired about a full-time job with p4p in Wilmington when her sentence was up, but he was not yet sold on her complete rehabilitation. There was something, he said, about the lack of emotion in her voice that didn't quite ring true. He had hastened to add that he might well be mistaken. He just could not yet get a true feel for her. In any case, there was time. She was not eligible for parole for four years.

After Allison had finished her redemptive recitation, Terry thanked her for all the work she was doing and nodded toward the first two handlers and their dog waiting by the door. It was time for a demonstration of the training progress.

First up was Jock, an eighty-pound chocolate Lab. Jock had entered the prison pipeline eighteen months ago as a skittish rescue dog and was now well on his way to becoming a model

Assistance Dog destined to be placed, given his size, with a combat veteran suffering from PTSD. He was, in fact, one of the three dogs Terry was transporting back to Wilmington that night to begin Public Access training in malls and movie theaters, at ball games and public parks.

Jock was led into the room by his senior trainer and her apprentice. On command—"Light, Jock, light!"—he ran over to the room's light switch, balanced himself on his hind legs, and with his front right paw turned it off, waited for a verbal prompt, and turned it back on. Then, at a second command—"Alert, Jock, alert!"—he scampered to a makeshift "alert button" constructed from a red rubber ball cut in half and taped to the wall and pushed it repeatedly. Meanwhile, whenever anyone came within five feet of his senior trainer, Jock had been taught to issue a "personal boundary bark" without prompting. The bark was more of a super loud "WOOF," and it struck me that big Jock would never have to give it twice. After responding successfully to each command, the Lab was showered with "good boys" and rewarded with a treat—what the literature calls a positive reinforcement training regimen.

Jock was followed by the eight-month-old Harper, a handsome white Labradoodle. Harper had been a gift from a Virginia breeder, the only such breed p4p had ever trained, and Terry was curious to see if the dog could combine a Poodle's intelligence with a Labrador's innate temperament to please. If so, Terry had a wheelchair-bound client, a young boy suffering from multiple sclerosis, in mind for the dog. Harper did not disappoint.

His two inmate handlers led him into the room acting as clients with physical disabilities, one using a cane and the other in a wheelchair. In his two months at Hazelton, they said, Harper had been a top student, and he began by opening and closing the cell door, using his front paws to lever the handle into place. Next he picked up and returned the cane that one of the handlers had dropped, and then he physically braced her as she "limped" across the room. I thought of Emilia Bartlinski.

Now the handler in the wheelchair took over, and when she dropped an empty soda can, Harper managed to maneuver it between his teeth ("get it") and deposit it into a garbage bin ("now trash"). Kyria had once told me that mastering wheelchair techniques and etiquette requires an Assistance Dog to respond to many more commands than, say, a psychological Service Dog must learn, and now one of Harper's trainers took a seat holding a set of flash cards behind her back. Wordlessly, she produced a card that read "sit." Harper sat. She showed "down," and he laid flat on his belly at her feet. She chose "stand," and he rose. "Shake" was followed by an extended paw. ("Good skill for children who can't speak well," Terry whispered in my ear.) It was only after the trainer allowed me to flash the cards to Harper—and I mixed up the order—that I was convinced there was not some crazy magician's sleight of hand at work.

As the dogs performed, I wondered how many repetitions it had taken Harper to learn to recognize the different shapes of the letters on those flash cards or for Jock to push that red alert button without becoming distracted. When I asked the head trainer, she told me that it had taken both dogs anywhere from three to six months, practicing every day, to perfect the tasks. "But keep in mind," she'd added, "all the dogs you're seeing today are probably our best pupils."

Including Morgan, whose turn it now was. Harper was a tough act to follow, but Morgan did not falter. The eight-month-old Golden Retriever was another "reader," and he began by following the commands "sit" and "down" as one of his trainers wrote them on a blackboard. Morgan's second handler had commandeered the wheelchair, and when she feigned a sort of seizure by shaking in the chair and finally slumping over, the dog ran to push the "alert button" before returning to her side and nuzzling her. Next, on command, Morgan turned the lights on and off and searched the room to retrieve a cell phone one of his handlers had hidden under a blanket. ("Phone, Morgan.")

"And what if Morgan happens to be placed with, say, a veteran who lives alone and depends on his meds to get him through a rough patch?" Morgan's trainer asked—and answered her own question with the command, "Meds, Morgan, meds!"

The dog ran to a refrigerator in the corner of the room, used his teeth to tug open the door by means of a length of rope attached to its handle, and brought the trainer a small bottle labeled "medicine." He then returned to the refrigerator to push the door closed.

On it went. Dogs reacting to laser pointers glowing on light switches or waking up a "sleeping" client having a nightmare. Dogs removing a "paralyzed person's" socks and gloves and depositing them in a laundry basket, or finding "lost" objects like sets of keys. When one black Labrador even dialed 9-1-1 on a toy telephone with oversized buttons, I half expected him to also open the refrigerator and grab me a cold beer.

Part of the paws4prisons curriculum is to master public speaking; Terry and Kyria feel that this skill not only promotes the self-assurance the inmates need to train their dogs but also serves a deeper psychological purpose of helping them to better understand, and move beyond, their criminal pasts. So between demonstrations, Lisa asked several of the handlers to recount their personal stories. The women—bank robbers, money launderers, murderers from states spanning the country, including one drug dealer from Albania—went into graphic detail about rapes, about seedy drug dens, about jabbing filthy needles into their arms.

Finally, late in the day, a thirty-something inmate appeared at the cell door. Lisa motioned her to enter, and she eased herself into the room with small, tentative steps, looking like she feared someone was going to jump out and strike her. She was clad in khakis but wore no yellow vest. Her face was like a hard winter breaking up, and two heavy satchels of flesh hung under her eyes, as if she'd been crying. Lisa whispered to me that she had been expelled from the program and was here to beg Terry to take her back.

The inmate told her story in a halting vibrato. Before her arrest a year ago, she said, she had been a stripper, a thief, and a drug dealer. She had been convicted of conspiracy to distribute methamphetamine and sentenced to sixty-five months.

"All through my teens, I had boyfriends who beat me and raped me," she said and began to sniffle. "I worked at a strip club, and when I was nineteen, I had my first child, the cutest little boy. His father was one of my customers. He disappeared. I don't know where he is.

"By the time I was twenty-two, I was addicted to meth," she said. "I used the needle a lot. I was still stripping; dancing and shooting, shooting and dancing. In the next three years, I had four abortions. I couldn't cope with the idea of bringing another child into my world.

"When they arrested me and sent me here, well, I thought this dog training was the best thing that ever happened to me. I was only an apprentice. But it really gave me some purpose." Here she began flat-out crying hard. One of the inmates handed her a tissue. "And it made me really happy."

After a few deep breaths she said, "But I screwed it up. I always screw it up. Bad old habits, you know?"

One night around Christmas, she continued, a group of tough inmates who knew she'd been a stripper asked her to pole dance in their cell. "I was scared. I didn't know what to do. I'm so sorry. I'm so sorry."

I could barely understand her through her sobs. She must have said "I'm so sorry" a dozen times.

When Lisa Christmas discovered her transgression, she booted her from the paws4prisons program. Now she had been allowed one last chance to ask to be let back in. Terry had sat silently as she recounted her story. When she finished and he still said nothing, the inmate continued to weep.

During our drive up to Hazelton, Terry had told me that the lessons he'd learned from dealing with the prisoners' emotional and psychological disabilities formed an early template for how paws4people approached its military clients. There was true concern and compassion in his voice when he guessed that between 70 to 80 percent of the female inmates he'd met over the years suffered from some form of PTSD.

"Some of them," he'd said, "rival the worst disorders afflicting our most battered combat troops."

If this poor woman wasn't one of those, I thought now, then who is? I also wondered if he would direct that compassion toward this teary-eyed stripper standing before him. Or would he be a hard-ass?

"One more chance," he said finally. "I don't even know why."

I think I do. Before we departed, Lisa and the inmates left Terry and me alone in the cell for a few moments while they arranged for a final dog line-up to say goodbye. I asked him flat-out why he appeared so heartless. Had he no empathy or compassion for these inmates? Did he not believe in second chances?

"Of course I believe in second chances," he said. His voice

was soft, thoughtful. "And sometimes third chances and fourth chances. I'm as loyal as a bulldog, and I'll stay with people until it's absolutely impossible to stay with them any longer. Because I've seen people come back from multiple screwups. How many screwups did I have in my life until I got to here? And we're talking major, major ones.

"Let me tell you something. That stripper. You know why I let her back? Because Lisa called me a couple of days ago and asked me to. She felt something in her gut about that gal, and she felt that another chance would be important for her development, her growth, whatever you want to call it. And I don't know that inmate from Adam, but I trust Lisa. So I went with Lisa's gut.

"The truth is, I have a hard time believing anybody on the initial pass. I don't know if that's a part of my makeup or a result of what I've been through. Maybe a little of both. You know the adage, actions speak louder than words? I tend to go by that more than anything else. So I'm sorry, but first they have to prove to me they're worth that extra chance. That gal couldn't prove anything to me with her words, but Lisa can, because of her actions and interactions with paws4people. Right or wrong, I go through life with what I hope is a healthy skepticism, and I try like hell not to let that skepticism slide into cynicism."

Here Terry fell silent. He looked around the room, at the blackboard with the written commands, and the fake alarm button taped to the wall, and the refrigerator with the rope hanging from its handle. He bent to stroke Chaeney and looked up at me.

"Sometimes I fail," he said after a minute.

"I hear so many stories about how these inmates want to change. But talk is cheap. The follow-up is what matters. The head trainer, the woman who said she wants to come work for us when she gets out. I've had probably one hundred prisoners say the exact same thing. Lots and lots of them are out now. And how many followed up? Two. David Burry and CeCe Miller."

Lisa returned, and as we exited the cell, the dogs and their handlers were lined up in a row, as if standing for a parade-ground inspection. Terry paused before each and thanked them. The pole dancer was among them; her eyes were red-rimmed, but she wore an embarrassed smile. Terry merely nodded.

After Lisa escorted us through the final prison gate, she and Terry made arrangements for his next visit, and before turning to walk back inside, she mouthed the words, "Thank you."

I knew she was talking about the pole dancer.

"Honest to God, Lisa, one inch. One inch out of line, out she goes. For good."

Lisa sort of grinned, and even Terry had to crack a smile. "Yes, sir, *General*," she replied with a crisp salute.

Then, to me, "See you at the Bump in eight weeks."

Chapter Six

Volunteers of Virginia

Puppy number six arrives at 3:33 a.m. Another male.

"This is getting spooky," Terry says. "We've never had six boys in a row like this."

Terry finishes his snipping and clipping and hands me the pup. Jackson—named after the South Carolina army base—is another plumper, weighing in at an even pound and a half, a smidge less than Lawson and Myer. I tie a mint green length of yarn around his neck and ask Kyria about the white blaze, like a horse's, running across the pup's forehead.

"A lot of them are born with that," she says. "Turns gold as they grow older."

The blaze is not Jackson's only distinction. A few months earlier, an Atlanta-based nonprofit group called the Heroes First Foundation—dedicated to easing the psychological and emotional suffering of military veterans and first responders—reached out to paws4people and pledged to donate the approximately $100,000 it costs to house, feed, insure, and cover three of the litter's medical needs over the eighteen to twenty-six months of training it takes to become a certified Assistance Dog. On a hunch, Terry and Kyria decided then and there that Jackson would be one of them. (The other two were chosen days later.)

The foundation could only hope that all or some of the dogs would eventually be placed with a combat vet in need of a canine companion, but of course p4p could not guarantee that. The dogs would naturally have to show an aptitude for the job during their training. Moreover, even if one or two or all three did exhibit that aptitude, this did not mean that Heroes First would be allowed to designate the recipient. Not even Terry or Kyria can do that. For, as in the case of Emilia Bartlinski and all the others, the foundation can present several candidates, but the decision will be left up to the dog itself.

The Heroes First Foundation's chairman of the board, John Kahran, owns a pipe-welding and water-meter SVP pump business near Atlanta, and one of his salesmen is Doug Mitchell, the father of the Iraq War veteran Jeff Mitchell. Three years ago, when Kahran learned of Jeff's struggles with PTSD and his involvement with paws4vets, he organized a fund-raising golf tournament in the shadow of Georgia's famous Stone Mountain to benefit paws4people and several other service-related charities. Thus was born Heroes First, and the tourney has become an annual event. For a small organization like p4p, the $100,000 donation was a boon.

In the United States alone, there are 1.6 million nonprofits of all stripes vying for charitable contributions, including at least two dozen Service Dog organizations whose operating budgets dwarf p4p's. A vast majority of these outfits have assets north of $5 million—in some cases, well north—and the quest among the dog groups for donations is more cutthroat than most people realize. By now it has probably dawned on you that as far-thinking and professional as Terry and Kyria may be, corporate ruthlessness is not an arrow in their quiver. In fact, they have too often relied on the "God will somehow provide" business model.

Further, unlike big and famous nonprofits—think the Red Cross or the Wounded Warrior Project—paws4people does not pull in a steady stream of small contributions from the general public. Once paws4people was certified as a local charity with the office of the government's Combined Federal Campaign, more money began arriving, including almost $70,000 worth of donations from federal employees last year. In addition, there are some loosely confederated associations that help keep it afloat—the army JAG wives of Washington, DC, for instance, are usually good for a few thousand dollars a year. But for most of its existence, p4p has relied on its own clients not only to raise its public profile via stories run in their local newspapers and television stations but also to generate funds to meet its annual nut, which currently reaches several hundred thousand dollars.

One evening early in my relationship with Terry, he arranged for two of p4p's more voracious fund-raising volunteers, Sonny Morrow and Rachael Wessell, to join me for dinner. Sonny is a Vietnam veteran with whom p4p had placed a mobility Assistance Dog. Rachael, a twenty-eight-year-old graphic designer, also has a mobility Assistance Dog. She was born with cerebral palsy that has confined her to a wheelchair her entire life.

"But don't tell her that she's got a disability," Terry advised me. "She even revels in her nickname, 'Wheels.'"

When I arrived at the restaurant, Rachael and her parents, Henry and Andie, were already seated. Rachael's speech is somewhat halting due to her condition, but she certainly lived up to Terry's contention. "I suppose *technically* I have cerebral palsy," she told me. "But that's not how I look at my world. I just consider myself someone who gets around differently."

Which aside from her wheelchair, she added proudly, included one hour a week of therapeutic horseback riding. I was stooping to say hello to her Service Dog, Dawson, a gorgeous Golden Retriever, when his ears shot up and his head swiveled toward the entrance. I followed his gaze and saw a handsome woman enter the room, followed by a large man on a motorized scooter with a mane of thick, close-cropped white hair and eyes the color of storm clouds. Trotting at Sonny Morrow's side was his Service Dog, Jake, a big black Labrador. Jake was wearing a stabilizing bar-harness contraption over his p4p vest, a device Sonny uses to balance himself.

The sixty-nine-year-old Sonny introduced his wife, Peggy, and then himself. He was one of p4p's earliest military clients, and his tone suggested an unspoken *the* before his name. A former army scout, he spent his career in the service despite tripping a land-mine during the Vietnam War that left bits of shrapnel embedded in his right knee. Rachael and Sonny and their families knew each other well, and as they all hugged hello, it struck me that the scene embodied what I was coming to recognize as paws4people's all-for-one, one-for-all ethos.

Take Rachael. She had met Dawson almost two years earlier and Bumped with him five months ago at Hazelton. Andie and Henry told me that despite her brave front, before Dawson's arrival, they sometimes felt as if their daughter's blithe spirit had been imprisoned in her unresponsive flesh. Rachael's business, for instance, revolves around designing logos for nonprofit organizations, but she could go nowhere, do no shopping, and take no meetings without either her parents or other caregivers hovering over her. Dawson has helped her break those invisible chains.

Dawson accompanies Rachael everywhere she travels, and though she does not drive—although she joked that when Google's self-driving car is rolled out, she expects Dawson to master its controls—she can now shop, dine, or meet potential clients by herself knowing that he has her back. Rachael tends to drop many things because of her pernicious impairment, and Dawson is always there to retrieve them. He even carries groceries to the supermarket checkout line, digs into his doggie pack with his teeth, and slides a credit card across the conveyer belt. Rachael also requires assistance dressing and undressing, and Dawson has learned to help her disrobe. "He's especially good with coats and socks," she said.

But just as important, Rachael told me, is the emotional companionship Dawson provides. "Before he came along, I always tried to stay positive about life. But I have to admit, sometimes everything just wore me down, mentally and physically. Now I have more energy than ever before."

As a result, she said, since being paired with Dawson, she has devoted much of her spare time to lobbying her hometown businesses, from malls to pizza parlors, to sponsor paws4people events. Her efforts have brought thousands of dollars to the organization. Such is her zeal that she recently put together a database to keep track of every single individual who donates to p4p in order to personally write each one a thank-you note on a card she designed herself. Given her physical disability, this is a painstaking labor of love.

"But you want to talk about fund-raising," she said with a giggle and pointed to Sonny. "There's the king."

At this, Sonny emitted a booming guffaw that caused other diners to peek over their shoulders. "Oh, no, no, no; I don't think so," he said. "Just trying to do my bit. Or, in this case, my two bits."

He let loose another cannon burst of laughter, and his wife Peggy groaned at the pun.

Sonny told me that after setting off the land mine, he faced a

long, slow recovery at various VA hospitals. But in time his rehabilitation had progressed sufficiently to allow him to resume his
army career, and he rose to the rank of colonel before he retired.
But his wounded knee, he said, never really stopped aching, and
ten years ago it finally gave out. He had the knee replaced, but his
mobility was further compromised when he was diagnosed with a
neurological disorder in both legs that makes walking difficult.

"We were at wit's end about what to do," Peggy said. "Sonny
was almost completely immobile. Then we heard about
paws4vets."

Sonny nodded. "If you just want to sit at home and die, that's
your right," he said. "I didn't want that to happen to me."

He hooked a thumb toward Jake, lying beneath the table next
to Rachael's Dawson. "This guy made sure it didn't."

Sonny does not like to talk about his donations to paws4peo-
ple, but I finally dragged out of him the amount of his latest tri-
umph, a gift of more than $4,000 he'd raised with his church
group. "I have another fund-raising project in mind," he said. "But
that's between me and Jake until it actually comes off."

We lingered over dinner, trading p4p stories until, toward the
end of our meal, Sonny rose from his seat and lifted his glass of
ginger ale. He offered a toast "to the absent Terry and Kyria." As
he stood, his legs buckled. Jake leaped to his feet and braced him,
leaning all his weight against Sonny's right knee. Sonny grinned
and finished the toast with one hand gripping the handlebar pro-
truding from Jake's harness.

Jake did not leave Sonny's side for the remainder of the meal.

"Dog's been a wonder," Sonny said. "Like he reads my mind."

As paws4people expanded, the fund-raising efforts of individuals like Rachael and Sonny—all the bake sales, car washes, and

fun runs that kept the outfit solvent in its early years—have been supplemented by larger grants from outfits like the Heroes First Foundation. Two years ago, p4p edged past six figures in donations for the first time, in large part because of a grant from the Purple Heart Foundation and a monetary gift from the Texas philanthropist Arthur Benjamin. Benjamin is a dog-loving marketing and advertising executive who adopted his own rescue dog and had it certified as a Service Dog by p4p. He was so taken by Terry and Kyria's vision that he decided to make his grant annual and requested that at least some of his grant funds be spent on supporting p4p's shelter-dog rescue operation.

But money is not everything. And long before Arthur Benjamin or the Purple Heart Foundation or John Kahran and Heroes First entered the p4p picture, Terry and Kyria built a network of volunteers centered in northern Virginia that were, and to some extent remain, the core of the organization. These are the people—some of them mental health professionals, others just big-hearted "citizens" who have their dogs certified by p4p as Therapy Dogs and either employ them in their practices or, in the case of the nonprofessionals, keep alive the tradition of visiting nursing homes, special ed classes, hospitals, and children's reading libraries. To a great extent, it is these volunteers who remain the organization's core mission.

Though paws4people may have moved its headquarters nearly four hundred miles south from the Virginia suburbs to the North Carolina coast, in a very real sense the outfit's soul still resides in the place where it was born. Thus, a few weeks after my prison runs with Terry, I scheduled a trip to Loudoun County, Virginia.

Allison Kaminsky, paws4people's director of canine operations in northern Virginia, wears her hair in a blonde bob, has
an infectious giggle, and brims with a kinetic energy. Before I
met her, Terry had described her to me as "perky." It was an
understatement.

Allison was my tour guide through Loudoun County, and on
my first Sunday morning in town, she filled me in on how she'd
fallen into p4p's orbit five years earlier. Having earned her bachelor of science degree in nursing, she was working in a local pedi-
atric hospital when one day she and her Golden Retriever Max
stopped by a "pet fiesta" being held in a neighborhood park. The
first booth she saw was operated by an outfit called paws4people.
She had never heard of it. Perusing the literature laid out on the
counter, she began talking with the man running the stand. It was
Terry. By the end of their conversation, she had signed up as a
volunteer.

"I love working with the kids in the hospital," she said. "And
when Terry described his visits to the special needs classes, well,
I was in. It was kind of a probationary deal at first. You know
Terry, he has to make sure people work well with his dogs. I think
what cemented it was when he watched me crawl through an
obstacle course with Addie and a bunch of special ed students
while wearing a skirt, blazer, and panty hose."

Allison enrolled Max in a p4p training program, and after he
was certified as a Therapy Dog, she began taking him along on
school visits. Max and Addie got on well, and meanwhile, Allison
and Terry became intrigued when special ed teachers mentioned
that some students lagging in their literacy programs showed steady
reading improvement when the dogs were present. Terry, Kyria, and
Allison put together a prospectus, and thus was born p4p's Reading
Education Assistance Dogs program, or R.E.A.D. In time the pro-

gram expanded from special ed classes to accommodate any and all students whose parents requested the help.

"It's good to have a furry-eared, four-pawed *friend* who will not judge you when you go off to do some one-on-one reading work," Allison explained. "Dogs don't poke fun at you if at first you can't sound out the words. They don't embarrass you in front of your peers by laughing at your mispronunciations. We call the dogs our Literacy Mentors, and since we can't bring them into a lot of the regular classrooms, our weekend library programs are the next best thing."

Which was why that morning Allison, Max, and I were heading to the Purcellville Public Library, where she had scheduled a children's reading event. The library is one of five in Loudoun County that has embraced the R.E.A.D. program, and it was mere coincidence that I was visiting on the day that Allison also planned, per paws4people's bylaws, to recertify seven Educational Assistance Dogs whose owners had volunteered them for the event.

Unlike most Service Dog providers, p4p's animals are tested periodically to ensure that they have retained the skills for which they were trained. Assistance Dogs with greater responsibilities, usually those placed with clients—a psychological Service Dog for Jeff Mitchell, for instance, or Sonny Morrow's and Rachael Wessell's mobility Service Dogs—must be recertified each year. Educational Assistance Dogs taking part in the R.E.A.D. program are recertified every three years. Should any dog repeatedly fail its tests, p4p's lend-lease arrangement allows Terry and Kyria to defrock them, so to speak.

When we reached the library, we found the seven p4p volunteers, all women, gathered with their dogs in the parking lot. Allison began by checking off the list of items each is required to carry whenever the dogs venture out to work. No one had forgotten to pack water and water bowls, hand sanitizers and towels (to clean spills), brushes, extra leashes, and "fetch items" (which included a preponderance of squeaky toys), or treats and poop baggies.

I thought it a bit incongruous when Allison rewarded each dog with a Froot Loop. It struck me that it was the handlers who deserved the treat. But she explained that she was testing the dogs to make certain that they "gummed" the tiny bit of cereal held loosely between her thumb and forefinger. Because these dogs work so closely with children, had any dog used its teeth instead of its lips and tongue to snatch the treat, she would have failed it. None had.

Allison would conduct more tests later in the day, predominantly to determine each dog's ability to obey basic commands and to remain gentle around the children. Should any flunk, she said as we filed into the library, she would temporarily suspend its Educational Assistance Dog certification until the dog was retested. No northern Virginia volunteer, she added, had ever had her dog recalled "to the home office."

Inside the library, at the entrance to a good-size reading room that had been set aside for this morning's Paws to Read event, a volunteer distributed doggie finger puppets crocheted with the words "Read to Me" while a dozen or so children between the ages of five and eight awaited us with their parents. Each child would take a turn reading to the eight dogs, including Max, clad in their orange Educational Assistance Dog vests. These children were not special needs students, merely kids whose parents and teachers felt that they needed "the extra work," as one mother of a second-grader told me.

"It relaxes my boy at the same time it pumps up his confidence that he can pronounce and understand the words," she said. "In school the teacher doesn't often have the time to give every child special attention. And though we read with our son at home whenever we can, having the dogs to read to makes it a little less like a chore and a little more fun."

Some of the kids approached the animals cautiously. "I'm a little scared of dogs," said one five-year-old girl whose cornrows were festooned with pink ribbons that matched the color of her dress.

Yet despite her initial fear, the little girl was soon sitting on the floor beside a stately Labrador slowly sounding out the words to Dr. Seuss's *One Fish, Two Fish*. Next to her a boy ran his index finger under the sentences of a Scooby-Doo mystery as he read them aloud to a patient Golden Retriever. Yes, the children made mistakes with some words, which their parents gently corrected. No, none of the animals laughed at those mistakes. Finishing a book earned each child a T-shirt adorned with a caricature of a Retriever with three thought bubbles over his head: "Sit," "Stay," "Read."

When a young boy named Jacob had finished his Spider Man comic, he told me, "When I read to the doggie, the words come easier."

He was no older than six, and when I glanced over his head, I saw his parents nodding and smiling. I thought of Liam-Antoine. My son is a kind and gentle boy, and from the time he could toddle, he has had a way with animals. As a youngster, he always said he wanted to be a veterinarian when he grew up—until, alas, we discovered he had inherited his father's decidedly nonmathematical genes. How much, I thought, he would have loved these dogs.

The scene in that library also brought to mind the long hours Liam-Antoine and I spent together as he learned to read and write

English. French may have been my son's first language, but he has been exposed to English from birth. To his mother's credit, she also saw the benefits of our son growing up bilingual.

His hometown of Aix-en-Provence, in the south of the country near Marseilles, is a favored destination for foreigners who either want to learn French or brush up on it with refresher courses. With that in mind, I proposed to Liam-Antoine's mother that she and he move into a three-bedroom apartment. The plan was to rent out the spare bedroom at below-market rates to visiting students whose first language was English, on the condition that they agreed to babysit a couple of nights a week and speak only English. We enrolled with a local travel agent who specialized in placing foreign students, I helped finance the apartment, and soon enough a string of Irish, English, American, Canadian, and Australian visitors were helping to improve my boy's English skills.

The final hurdle was to enroll Liam-Antoine in a private school just outside of Aix in which, from grades five through twelve, half the courses are taught in English. The school—which most everyone refers to incongruously as The American School despite the fact that most of the teachers are from the United Kingdom—has a rigid bilingual entrance examination. I was confident Liam-Antoine would pass the orals. The English language reading and writing tests, not so much. And that's how he came to live with me to attend fourth grade in the States.

It was hard on us both at first, on so many levels. He spoke English so well that his teachers assumed he could also read and write it. But he had, at best, a rudimentary grasp of the written language. I remember well spending hour upon hour at our kitchen table each night, trying to cram years of reading and writing curricula into a couple of fourth-grade semesters. It was a grinding experience, and at times I felt terrible for the boy when he would stumble over the same mispronunciation—"Yes, in English you always pronounce the *S* at the end of a word"—or quirk in our language. *"I" before "E" except after "C"?*

It was dizzying. But he hung in there and, in the end, proved an adept student.

Observing those children in the Purcellville Public Library reading to p4p's Educational Assistance Dogs, I could not help but recall those long, frustrating nights for Liam-Antoine, and what I wouldn't have given to know then what I know now about the power of canines to ease that frustration. I sure could have used one of those dogs around the house.

As it turned out, when Liam-Antoine returned to France, he passed The American School's reading and writing entrance examinations. He is seventeen as I write this, about to enter his senior year of high school and looking into colleges in England, Scotland, and Ireland. If he ends up choosing a university where the professors speak either with a thick Highlands burr or an indecipherable Belfast accent, I may have to ship him over one of p4p's dogs after all.

The week I spent in northern Virginia turned into something of a whirlwind tour, as Allison had packed my schedule tight with all manner of meetings, interviews, and events. I spent a morning in a local special needs kindergarten class with a p4p volunteer whose two Therapy Dogs, both Golden Retrievers, helped four boys afflicted with various levels of autism learn to count to ten.

"It may not look like much," their teacher told me, "but most of these boys just won't open up to a human the way they will to a dog."

And one evening I dined with three p4p volunteers—an ICU nurse, a Loudoun County medical case manager, and the administrator for a local volunteer rescue squad—who regaled me with stories of their Therapy Dogs brightening the lives of patients they visited at hospices and nursing homes. While we ate and talked, the three dogs lay silently beneath the restaurant table.

One afternoon Allison and I drove to a coffee shop to meet her friend Shannon DeLacy, whom Allison had known since grade school. Shannon's eight-year-old son Jack was born with a mitochondrial disorder that leaves him with the physical and mental functionality of an infant. At Allison's urging, Shannon and her husband applied for a p4p Service Dog, which Jack had already Bumped with and was scheduled to arrive soon.

"Jack doesn't really understand what's wrong with him," Shannon told me, "and we're hoping a dog—as a friend and companion—can assuage some of that confusion."

She added that Jack has just begun to train with a walker, but because he also suffers from seizures, she and her husband plan to attach handles to the Service Dog's vest—à la Sonny Morrow's Jake—not only to speed up Jack's learning curve but also to give them another set of eyes to watch over the boy.

"Allison swears a dog will change Jack's life," Shannon told me with a brave smile. "We only pray to God that she's right."

But of my many experiences in Virginia, two bear repeating in detail. The first involves Elaine Johnson, an animal-assisted therapist. Elaine is the therapist-in-residence at a private, nonprofit health care facility in Leesburg, Virginia, that offers counseling and psychiatric care to children suffering from a raft of disabilities, ranging from autism to substance abuse to intellectual and developmental syndromes. The forty-ish Elaine was tall and thin, wore her blonde hair cropped short, and on the day we met in her office, she was dressed casually in a black turtleneck and khaki trousers. She owned the two Service Dogs lolling at her feet, the playful four-year-old Golden Retriever Willson and the nine-year-old chocolate Labrador Molly.

"Professionals by day, pets by night," she joked.

Elaine had worked as a human resources manager in her native Cambridge, England, and as a physical therapist and personal trainer after immigrating to the States. Then, three years ago, she met Terry at an event similar to the "pet fiesta" where he'd encountered Allison. Terry, Elaine said, was immediately smitten with Molly. He invited them both to join him on school visits. Molly got on so well with the special needs children that Terry suggested Elaine enroll her in p4p's Therapy Dog program. Molly flew through the accreditation process, and Elaine took a job counseling emotionally disturbed children at a local parks and recreation facility. Not long after, the father of one of the kids she treated approached her about working at the Leesburg facility, which he owned. She jumped at it.

One of her first patients was an adopted fourteen-year-old girl, and as Elaine recalled her, she murmured, "Oh, what trouble."

"She had what's called reactive detachment disorder," she said. "Something terrible had happened to her early in her life; she was either neglected or abused or both, and we never found out. Her adoptive parents had placed her with us because she just would not socialize. When she arrived, she wouldn't go to class. Attacked the staff. Tried to run away whenever she could."

At this, Elaine shook her head and stooped low to cuddle Molly. It was clear that the memory moved her, maybe frightened her.

"Anyway, on top of all this, her personal hygiene was atrocious. She wouldn't bathe, her clothes were a mess, and she wouldn't wash her hair. So Molly and I would see her every day, twice a day, and I innately sensed a bond between her and the dog. I made up a game. If she would complete a certain amount of schoolwork by each session—English assignments, a math problem, spelling; really anything—she could pet Molly or brush her or feed her a treat.

"Suddenly she began showing up for her sessions in clean clothes and with her hair combed. Her teachers told me that she was doing all her homework and even interacting with the other students. Finally, there was a talent show the kids were putting on, and she asked me if she could learn a dance with Molly for the show. I gave her the music, I lent her Molly for rehearsals, and the two of them would practice in my office. She would take Molly's front paws in her hands, and they would do a happy little jig. She even taught Molly to kind of keep their 'dance steps' in sync. I suppose other dogs can perform like that, but I'd never seen anything like it.

"On the day of the talent contest," she said, "that girl stood up before the entire school and did her sort of freestyle canine dance with Molly. When they finished, they both took a bow. It was the most beautiful thing I have ever seen. She just blossomed like a flower."

Elaine guessed that Molly's nonjudgmental nature was the key to the transformation of the girl's personality. This, of course, is a theme running through the entire Assistance Dog community. Most professional Service Dog handlers are familiar with the theories put forth by researcher scientists like Duke University's Brian Hare and Vanessa Woods. But in the end, no one really *knows* for certain why dogs so connect with tortured and abused human minds and souls.

What Elaine Johnson did know is that Molly turned around this young girl's life.

The young teen, Elaine said, was released back to her adoptive mother and father a few months after the talent show. Elaine still receives progress reports, which describe the girl adapting well to her new home and school. And then there is the keepsake. Before the girl was released from the facility, she visited Elaine and Molly for one final therapy session. Toward the end, she presented Elaine with a poem she had written.

"I still carry it to this day," Elaine said, fishing through her briefcase. "To remind me of one of the most fantastic experiences that has ever happened to me."

She pulled out a sheet of lined paper fraying at its edges and handed it to me. The poem was entitled "Molly."

It read:

When times were tough
And I was acting a fool
I met you Molly and boy
Were you cool.
Times were hard, but you
Were there,
I started to give up, but then
You made me care.
The bad times passed
And we had fun,
We learned some tricks
To play and run,
I love you Molly
You're such a charm,
I trust you much
You never do harm.
I know when I leave

You'll be in my heart
I know Molly
Inside we'll never part

When I finished reading it aloud, Molly barked.

───────────────

But what about the dogs?

If Terry's theory of dogs absorbing and internalizing a human's misery is valid—and reams of anecdotal evidence suggest that there is something to it—does that not constitute some kind of cruel and unusual punishment for these poor creatures?

Sandi Dettra answered that question for me. Sandi is another professional dog whisperer, a substance abuse therapist for the Grafton Integrated Health Network, a nonprofit organization that operates three behavioral health care centers for children and adults across northern Virginia. Sandi treats kids with drug problems, and when Allison set up our meeting, she'd mentioned that Sandi had a rather harrowing tale involving her Service Dog, Phin.

So I arrived curious the next afternoon when I met Sandi in her small office adjacent to her session room. She worked out of an old farmhouse that served as headquarters for one of the Grafton institutions. She introduced Phin as her "assistant."

"Watch out," she warned as the rather massive black Labrador jumped up to lick my face. "Phin's a kisser."

Like many drug counselors—all drug counselors?—Sandi had the blasé mien of a person who had seen and heard every trick in the book. I felt that if I told her that her long, blonde hair was on fire, she would calmly rise from her seat, saunter to a nearby wall mirror to check, and casually find a faucet to run over her head. It comes, I suppose, with the profession. In an occupation where people are continually lying, the term *face value* takes on new meaning.

Four years ago, Sandi said, she had come across a newspaper article about paws4people and called Allison out of the blue with a request: She was interested in acquiring a dog that she could use as a narcotics sniffer.

"You know, go to the dorms, check the kids, make sure things are clean."

Although this was a new one for p4p, Allison helped Sandi find a breeder who sold her the puppy Phin. Thereafter Sandi and Phin worked with a professional narcotics dog trainer while also, at Allison's strong urging, agreeing to place Phin in p4p's Therapy Dog training program.

Phin had a full year of both narcotics and therapy training under his leash when he finally joined Sandi at work at the institution. He proved a natural, not only as a drug sniffer but also as one of those animals who somehow formed a bond with the most troubled teens in Sandi's program. If one of the adolescents broke down in tears during group therapy sessions — it happened often, Sandi said—Phin would approach the child and lay his head on her lap. As she put it, "You could almost see the anxiety draining from the kid.

"Phin is just so in tune with them it's scary," she said. "I've got some shattered teenagers in here. They're drug addicts, yes, but they also suffer from depression, anxiety, bipolar disorder. A lot of the girls have been raped. And Phin just seemed to sense who needed what. We've got one boy with Asperger's syndrome who doesn't have a lot of friends; the kids think he's obnoxious, and he can be. Phin loves him. I think the dog senses the other kids' dislike and fear. So Phin just crawls up into his lap and kisses him over and over."

This affection comes at a cost to Phin. He leaves many of Sandi's group sessions exhausted and listless, barely able to walk. This was never more evident, she said, than just last week, when a sixteen-year-old girl confined to Grafton overdosed during one of Sandi's group sessions.

"She'd gone home on a weekend pass and snuck some pills back in with her." Sandi shook her head. "How she got them through security? No clue.

"Anyway, the kids were all in the group room, and I kept looking at this girl, and I knew something was wrong with her. Now this girl is afraid of dogs and Phin knows that, so he keeps his distance. But that day, when she slumped in her chair and her eyes rolled into the back of her head, he knew he had to do something. We called the nurses and the EMTs, and while we waited, I hurried the rest of the group into another room. The other girls had a hard time watching this scene—that used to be them. Several of them reacted badly."

One girl became hysterical, Sandi continued; the gruesome scene had set off flashbacks. She crawled into a corner in the anteroom, balled up into the fetal position, and started wailing "from the pain of her emotional memories."

Sandi had remained with the overdosing girl, so Phin jumped into action. He approached the weeping girl, sat beside her, and began nuzzling her with kisses. She threw her arms around him and nearly squeezed the life out of him. But as she petted him over and over, her crying softened. When the tears stopped altogether, Phin left to check on Sandi.

"So Phin came back into the session room. He knew the girl overdosing was afraid of him, so he hid himself from her view behind the couch. He could see me and her, but she could not see him. And he'd just sit there for ten minutes, until he would hear the other girl crying again, and he'd run back into the anteroom to nuzzle with her again.

"This went on until help arrived. It was as if the dog was trying to emotionally rescue three people—me, the overdosing girl, and the crying girl. We finally got the girl with the drugs the medical help she needed. And after I calmed down the rest of the group, well, Phin and I both had to get out of there."

But that, Sandi said with a wan smile, "was not the kicker. When we got home, Phin went straight to his bed and did not, could not, move. I went out to the gym. I needed to work out my own thoughts and emotions. And when I got home from the gym, for the first time ever, Phin did not greet me at the door. He *always* hears my car pull in and runs to the front door. But he was just so tired. Completely done in. It took him three days to come back from that, to get back to normal. My heart just broke for him."

The girl who overdosed, Sandi said, had since been released from the hospital and returned to the institution. Her weekend passes had been revoked, and Sandi expected her back in group therapy sessions soon. She gazed down at her dog.

"That'll be interesting, won't it, Phin?" she said. I half-expected the animal to answer. Or flee.

◦•═══════════════•◦

On my last day in Virginia, I accompanied Allison to a local Home Depot, where she administered a p4p recertification test to a psych Service Dog in the store's noisy and crowded home-repair aisle. The dog was a Golden Retriever named Fallon who had been placed a year earlier with the former Air Force Major Mike

Branck. Mike had been medically discharged with a severe case of traumatic brain injury and PTSD.

It was fun watching Allison put the animal through its paces, many of which were similar to the garage training I'd witnessed back in Wilmington that morning with Kyria. Mike, for instance, told Fallon to sit and stay, and then he walked around a corner and out of sight. Despite the heavy traffic in the store, Fallon did not move until Mike returned. Another test involved Allison dropping her clipboard behind Fallon as the dog accompanied Mike down an aisle. Despite the loud bang inches from her rump, the dog never took her eyes off Mike.

Later over coffee, I enjoyed chatting with the shy, soft-spoken Mike. But I could not shake Molly's and Phin's stories from my memory.

Terry once told me that initially he wasn't completely sold on the idea of paws4people Service Dogs working with mental health professionals. He just did not think that the animals could form the same bond, and therefore have the same impact, as Service Dogs who were placed permanently with p4p clients.

Since then he has witnessed, and has been moved by, the life-changing effects that animals like Phin and Molly have had on people, particularly children. He has changed his tune. When I returned to my motel from the Home Depot, I called Terry. In what I am sure was a semicoherent rush of emotion, I poured out to him all I had seen and heard during my week in Virginia.

He listened patiently as I babbled on. Then, finally, I thought I detected a droll chuckle on the other end of the line.

"Yup," he said finally. "I think you're ready. See you at the Bump."

Chapter Seven

The Bump (1)

I t is almost 4:00 in the morning when April Cook arrives at the Wilmington headquarters. Kyria had phoned April when Claire went into labor, and she'd rushed over from Fayetteville as fast as she could. As April walks through the door, Claire's head swivels and her tail pounds the floor at the sight and scent of her "partner."

April is a slim, trim, and freckled thirty-something—redden her hair and style it in pigtails and she could pass for Raggedy Ann, right down to the surprised "O" her mouth makes when she bustles into the building. I suspect she is a bit startled by the crowd milling about the whelping room, the adjacent anteroom, even the kennel. But her concern for Claire's well-being overrides whatever trepidation she feels about all these strangers, and she makes a beeline for her dog.

With eyes glued to the floor, she brushes past Kyria, Renee, the students, and me, pausing only long enough to peck Terry on the cheek. I notice that she is the first of tonight's visitors to show more interest in the mother than the pups. She bends to greet Claire and looks back to Terry, conveying without words her anxiousness over her Assistance Dog's health. Terry gives her a thumbs-up, and April visibly relaxes. She hugs Claire tight for several moments before turning her attention to the newborns.

April has made great emotional strides since she teamed with Claire, but she still has an aversion to crowds, particularly crowds of strangers. David Burry had described for me his first day of Public Access training with April and Claire a few years earlier; they were in an Old Navy outlet packed with shoppers when a baby's squall pierced the store. April was already nervous, and the wail somehow stirred in her memories of Iraq. Her anxiety, in David's words, "spiked to a ten." She went immobile for a good ten minutes, down on bended knee, as David spoke softly to her, trying to snap her out of it. But it was only Claire's nuzzling presence, David said, that finally brought her back.

Since that experience, April's condition has improved considerably. Terry encouraged her to return to school, and with Claire by her side, she enrolled at Liberty University, where she recently received her master's degree in Christian counseling. As a sort of reward, Terry named her a "Peer Mentor" for paws4vets. It is, of course, a volunteer position, and she plans to concentrate on advocating for what Department of Defense surveys have found to be the half-million women in uniform who, like April, have been the victims of military sexual trauma, or MST.

According to the Pentagon, in the last year alone, reports of sexual assaults by members of the military rose by an unprecedented 46 percent, prompting the secretary of defense to declare the epidemic a "clear threat" to both male and female service members. The startling jump in reported cases has also triggered hearings on Capitol Hill, where lawmakers persistently question just how capable the services are of policing their own.

So far the Department of Defense has staved off efforts to hand over to civilian courts the prosecution of military sexual predators. The generals and admirals argue that they are capable of dealing with the problem within the military justice system. But as histories such as April's suggest, the Pentagon has far to go before it owns up to its own shortcomings. Unlike so many service members either shamed into silence or afraid for their careers, April was brave enough to step forward and accuse her superior officer of repeated sexual assaults. For this, she was threatened with a dishonorable discharge.

The fact that so many service members now feel empowered to report these crimes is heartening. But because the syndrome was buried for so long, the study and treatment of its military victims is a relatively new field. As a result, the placement of Assistance Dogs with MST victims lags far behind the proven benefit the animals have on former soldiers suffering from post-traumatic stress disorder and traumatic brain injury. Even the official stance of the Department of Veterans Affairs is that not enough clinical research has been done to determine if Service Dogs alleviate the symptoms of MST. This strikes many people as odd, considering that the VA does acknowledge that most veterans suffering from MST are also plagued by PTSD or TBI, if not both.

The symptoms of the three syndromes are similar, if not intertwined—nightmares, an aversion to public places, flashbacks, a fear of intimacy, even a violent aversion to uniforms. Shortly after her discharge, for instance, April was pulled over by a state trooper for having a broken taillight. As the officer approached her car, her body began to tingle and shake. By the time he let her off with a warning, she was falling into a full-blown flashback of her sexual assault in Iraq. A panic attack ensued, leaving her curled up in the fetal position in her front seat, her arms death-gripping the steering wheel.

But she has journeyed far from those days, and she knows it.

She recently learned that a female member of her navy unit had committed suicide after also being sexually assaulted. It was a turning point. No longer, she vowed, would she sit silent, nursing her own wounds. As she put it in a blog post that mourned the dead woman, "For a long time I may have shut out my fellow service members and friends. But in the future, with Claire's help, I would rather meet them at a dog playdate than visit with a stone slab."

To that end, she is in the process of relocating to Wilmington in order to be closer to the p4p headquarters and her new job of getting the word out that p4p is here to help fellow MST sufferers. Tonight it is almost as if Claire had been awaiting April's arrival. Within moments her milk begins to flow, and the puppy scrum at her teats intensifies. This presages by exactly four minutes another of this night's firsts. At 4:09 a.m. Claire gives birth to her seventh pup—at long last, a girl!

She will be named Shelby in honor of the army camp in Mississippi, and I will finally get to use the pink length of yarn I set aside four hours earlier.

As Kyria's students swarm the new female pup, April stays close to Claire, cuddling and cooing into her ear. Their bond reminds me of the very first time I met Terry at Fort Stewart and the Wounded Warrior Battalion commander's observation: "It's almost like there are electric currents coursing through the leashes, connecting the minds of the soldiers with the minds of their dogs."

According to Claire's sonogram, she has one more puppy to deliver, one more birth before she is home free, free to return to April. As I watch the two cuddle, I wonder what Claire saw in the mind of the tortured April that drew the dog to her.

Maybe the upcoming Bump will help explain it.

We were nearly snowed out. The blizzard had begun in earnest the previous night—a natural hazard in early March in West Virginia. Terry and Kyria worried over which of the new clients would actually make it to Morgantown. Flights into the city were at first delayed and finally cancelled and rerouted to Pittsburgh. But Terry and the half-dozen p4p volunteers who had caravanned up from North Carolina a day earlier organized a makeshift shuttle service to the Pittsburgh airport, 75 miles away. The usual 90-minute drive between the two cities became a dicey, hours-long slog across an arctic snowscape.

As it turned out, three of the four clients eventually arrived in Morgantown that night. The fourth—a twelve-year-old girl born with severe and permanent brain damage—was waylaid by the weather with her parents at the Charlotte, North Carolina, airport. Her Bump would be rescheduled.

When potential clients apply to paws4people for an Assistance Dog, an informal screening committee of Terry, Kyria, and a few longtime volunteers and trainers make the final decision via a combination of need, hunch, and exigency. At the moment, there are nearly one hundred applicants on the p4p waiting list who have been interviewed and approved to receive Service Dogs. And though the chosen sometimes fall into a first-come, first-served category, Terry and Kyria also take into account the personalities of the dogs who are ready to be placed. In today's case, they felt they had a nice mix—two veterans and two children—for the animals to choose from, although because of the blizzard one of the dogs would now have to wait.

Terry and Kyria recognized early on that integrating military veterans with disabled children both for Bumps and Public Access training sessions—"crossblending," Kyria calls it—has a salubrious effect on the vets. Many of the children are too young to realize that they are suffering from such horrendous impairments and syndromes, and they are usually overjoyed to be receiving a new friend and helpmate. The veterans see this and, as Terry puts it, "a sort of 'There but for the grace of God go I' mind-set kicks in.

"It puts things in perspective," he says. "Sure, they have it tough. But then they look at these kids and say, 'If that little girl with brain damage can feel total love when a dog jumps up in her lap and licks her and slobbers all over her; if that little boy in a wheelchair can smile and laugh through his pain, then, okay, I can at least try.'"

That time for trying was fast approaching. Before the sun was up the next day, a slow train of vehicles climbed through the snow fog to the plateaued peak of the craggy mountain and drove through the gates of Hazelton Federal Prison. Our group numbered close to forty, including clients and their families; a half dozen of Kyria's students (including some who had invited their parents); John "Miami" Phillips, p4p's Atlanta-based chief of staff and head fund-raiser; the still photographer Joan Brady, who donates her time; and the videographer Jim Gilson, a former CNN cameraman whom Miami had hired to tape the day's proceedings. Also among us was the eighteen-year-old Alex Keefover, a young man suffering from cerebral palsy who had Bumped with his Service Dog, the Golden Retriever Kingsley, over a year earlier.

Alex and his mom were here to retrieve Kingsley from a refresher course with the inmate handlers. The wheelchair-bound Alex, who like Rachael Wessell relies on his Service Dog to retrieve things he drops and to help him dress and undress, would be off to college in the fall to study meteorology (his dream was to work for the National Weather Service). Since college would be Alex's first extended time away from his parents, Terry and Kyria thought it prudent for Kingsley to brush up on his mobility training.

Once through the prison gates, our entourage was escorted into a large dining hall where long tables were laid out in concentric semicircles around a podium. The institution's twenty-one handlers filled the first two rows. Their dozen or so dogs sat at their feet sporting yellow p4p vests and yellow kerchiefs around their necks. In the back of the room the kitchen staff, also inmates, had put out urns of coffee, pitchers of orange juice, and fresh-baked muffins.

The prison vocation specialist and p4p administrator Lisa Christmas began the proceedings with a prayer and then introduced the handlers. Each stood and stated their names, their crimes, and their sentences. I watched the shock register in Kyria's students' eyes as the women confessed to dealing drugs, to running prostitution rings, to committing violent armed robberies.

When the last had finished her public confession, the inmates rose as one and surprised Lisa by reading a farewell poem they had penned. Lisa had recently announced her upcoming retirement, and after each inmate read a line from the poem, they presented her with a going-away present—a plaque with all the dogs' paw prints embedded in clay. She cried, as did many in the room. On its face the setting was fairly incongruous. Hardened criminals reciting poesy and presenting a hunk of clay to a prison administrator. But I felt I knew these women now, knew their hopes and dreams, knew how hard they were working to make up for their crimes and turn their lives around. I was moved.

Next came the dog demonstrations—vignettes similar to the scenarios I had witnessed here at Hazelton two months earlier. Golden Retrievers waking "PTSD sufferers" from nightmares. Labradors helping wheelchair-bound "clients" to load laundry into a washing machine. Both breeds retrieving "meds" from a refrigerator. When these concluded, Terry stood and strode to the center of the room to introduce his "special guest" Alex Keefover and Alex's mother, Jennifer.

Alex gave an embarrassed wave as his mother stood and beamed. Despite her beautiful smile, the lines on Jennifer Keefover's face hinted at the years of stress that comes with caring for a disabled child. As part of the Bump, Terry and Kyria require each client—or in the case of some children, one or both parents—to explain why they applied for an Assistance Dog. But neither Alex nor Jennifer had to address the room this morning. They had already fulfilled that task at Alex's Bump. Nonetheless, I sensed that Terry had asked Jennifer to say a few words in order to pave the way for the new clients who would soon have to rise and tell their stories.

Jennifer allowed that she was jittery, not just because of having to speak in public but also because she was nervous and worried about her son leaving home.

"The biggest challenge for Alex was—I guess still is—getting and maintaining his independence," she said. "And that's where Kingsley has stepped in. Hopefully, the plan is he'll be able to deal with that without Mom having to be there next year when he's at school."

I could read the hope on her face that this would be so as she looked toward the seated inmates and said, "You guys are the ones who started the whole thing. So thank you, all of you. On Alex's behalf. On our family's behalf."

Then she turned to Terry and Kyria. She opened her mouth, but no words came out. She sniffled and wiped her eyes, but she could not stop the tears. Terry walked up to her, hugged her, and walked her back to her seat beside her son.

As Jennifer, Alex, and Kingsley settled at a table in the back of the room, Terry again took the floor. He told the assembly that the next three clients he would introduce had been screened and chosen from among eighty-eight paws4people applicants.

"I wish we could satisfy them all," he said. Then in a wistful voice, "Maybe someday we will. But for now, I'd like you all to meet Josh Gregor and his mother, Tracey."

Nine-year-old Josh gripped his mom's hand tight as they stepped toward the podium. Josh walked stiffly, the complicated apparatus in his backpack that attaches to his body obviously hindering his movement. His father, Brian, who remained seated at their table, inconspicuously flicked away a tear while placing a protective arm around Josh's teenage sister, Elizabeth.

Tracey tentatively lifted the microphone from its stand, and Josh huddled in close to her skirt, much as I had seen Emilia Bartlinski do with her mom months earlier in Catonsville, Maryland.

Tracey pointed to Brian and Elizabeth and said, "Brian and I have been married for almost twenty-two years. We also have a twenty-year-old and a seventeen-year-old. Josh is our youngest, and we're here looking for a dog for him."

Then Tracey faced the prison inmates. "First of all to you ladies, I would like to say that I never expected to come here and get the blessings that we have gotten today. It's only by the grace of God that any of us are not in your seats and in your shoes. We all make mistakes. And I never expected to see such beautiful, lovely ladies in a prison. I want to thank you for the awesome job you are doing. You are going to touch a lot of lives."

The inmates beamed and Tracey went on, running her fingers through Josh's wavy brown mop as she spoke. "Joshua was born nine weeks early; he was taken by emergency C-section because he was almost gone. As it was, he spent the first six months of his life in ICU."

Josh, she said, was the victim of a genetic syndrome wherein a major section of his small bowel had twisted in on itself and turned gangrenous in utero. The bowel was removed upon his birth, and for his entire life Josh has been attached to the life-sustaining gastrostomy tube now hidden in the backpack he wore on his slim frame. Although Josh is able to ingest small snacks, he receives 100 percent of his daily nutrition via the tube inserted into his abdomen that delivers his food directly into his stomach. In addition, he had been born nearly deaf, and despite the cochlear implant in his left ear and the hearing aid on his right, he still has trouble communicating.

"He's had surgery on his throat to improve his breathing," Tracey said. "But his eyes are good and his heart is good. So when people ask me, 'What's wrong with Josh?' I'm like, 'Well, let me tell you what's not wrong with him. It's a lot quicker.'"

Josh threw his arms around his mother's leg. Everyone in the room smiled.

"As you can see," Tracey continued, "Josh is a little bit small for his age, but he goes to a regular school and sits in a regular third-grade classroom with the other children. But we've had some difficulty this year with him trying to keep up, and he has struggled a bit learning to read and write.

"But I am here to tell you that Josh is a good kid, a joy to have, and he's just been a big blessing. For all the heartache, God's always been there for us and taken care of us. Though some may pity us and think that it's awful, it really is a blessing. But it is hard to handle this by ourselves, so we are hoping to find a dog that can alert him. You see, his hearing is our main concern."

Once again I was struck by the spirituality running like an electric current through every aspect of paws4people. I confess that I can, at best, be described as a Deist. I suppose I have seen too many die on battlefields around the world in the name of religion. But I begrudge no one his faith—in particular the faith I saw the p4p clients rely upon to recognize and accept their physical, emotional, and psychological burdens. Religion was far from a crutch for these people. It was a saving grace, and the dogs of p4p are the blessing through which it is delivered. At least that was what I was beginning to understand as Tracey continued.

"Because of the background noise, Josh has trouble hearing in large rooms like this. This happens outside a lot, too. You try to get his attention, but he can't hear you. But let's face it, nine-year-old boys, no matter their afflictions, are still curious. So if he wanders away from me outside and gets near water or traffic, a dog to watch over him would be a blessing not only for his safety but also for his independence.

"But most of all, I think Josh just needs a best friend. You see, Josh is really insecure at night. When you're deaf and you have to close your eyes, you don't like for it to be dark. You want to be able to see what's going on. And so we have a light on in his room all the time. Plus, because of his condition, he often wakes up with a lot of abdominal pain and a lot of digestive problems. Also, he has problems with his feeding tube at night. It will kink up, which shuts down the pump's flow. When that happens, it sets off an alarm on the pump."

And here Tracey Gregor paused and sighed. "So you get up and reset it and start it over. That usually happens several times a night. We're hoping that the dog we get can wake Josh's dead-to-the-world mom from sleep to get things rolling again."

Tracey seemed to be at a loss for what else to say and looked down at her son and smiled. "So what else should I tell them, Josh?"

Shy Josh let go of his mother's leg and edged a few feet away toward the middle of the room. He held his head up straight, glanced at his father and sister, and took a deep breath. In a squeaky, high-pitched voice he said, "Thank you for the doggie. Thank you for people like you."

"What kind of dog do you want?" Tracey prodded her son.

"A Golden Retriever," he managed to blurt before scampering back to his mother's side and again wrapping his arms around her leg.

Tracey then thanked everyone again, bent down, and planted a tender kiss on Josh's forehead as Brian and Elizabeth rose and began clapping. Everyone followed their lead, and from the corner of my eye, I saw Terry stand and cross the back of the room. As the ovation reached its crescendo, he placed a hand on Tony Mullis's shoulder, leaned in, and whispered something into his ear.

The twenty-three-year-old former marine combat engineer Tony Mullis still wore his thick, blond hair in a military buzz cut. This lent his round and freckled face the appearance of someone much younger, perhaps Huck Finn lighting out for the territories. His long-sleeve "Ducks Unlimited" T-shirt emphasized the effect. Despite the snow and freezing temperatures, Tony had arrived at Hazelton in khaki cargo shorts. He did not have to worry about keeping his legs warm. He had none.

Tony rose from his seat; kissed his wife, Jeannie, and twenty-three-month-old son, Cason; and approached the podium with a pantherlike grace. It was as if he had been born with the two titanium prostheses extending from his shorts to his anklet socks and white New Balance sneakers. Tony's "legs" looked like shiny erector sets.

"How's everybody doing today?" he said in a drawl as thick as the red clay of his rural west Georgia hometown. And despite his aw-shucks demeanor, it struck me that addressing a crowd of strangers in this prison dining hall was probably the last place in the world Tony wanted to be. I had read Tony's paws4people application profile, and in it he had confessed to the anxiety that has plagued him since his medical discharge from the corps a year ago.

"In the marines there is always someone there to watch your back," he had written, "and that is what I am here to do for my wife and son. Now I need a friend that can do the same for me."

As he stood before us on his prosthetic legs, he explained that it had been nearly two years to the day since he'd stepped on an improvised explosive device, or IED, during his second deployment to the hellbroth that is Afghanistan's Helmand Province. I imagined this six-foot, 155-pound marine on patrol and decked out in full "battle rattle"—the fifty pounds or so of helmet, goggles, flak vest, rucksack, poncho, and weapons American fighting men carry into combat. I'd bet it felt lighter that day, given that he'd learned only a few hours earlier that Jeannie had given birth to a son. He had to have been joyous, maybe even boasting to his platoon mates.

Then came the IED blast—"my accident," Tony called it. As he lay in shock among his own blood and gore, he said, he could sense by the look on the navy corpsman's face that there was no chance of saving the limbs. His left leg had been blown off above the knee, his right leg below. Cason would never see his father whole.

"Today I have no problems walking; I don't hurt," he said, but then his face reddened and his mouth torqued into an uneasy smile. It was the smile of a man who had been taught to always speak the truth. Perhaps by his parents, certainly by the marine corps. A man who will teach his son the same.

"Well, okay, yes, it does kind of hurt; I'm not gonna lie about it," he continued, and stole a quick glance at his fake legs. "In fact, it kind of sucks putting them on every morning. But as you get on, as you push yourself every day, they feel more and more like your own. In truth, I've actually been pretty blessed when there are so many people I fought with who never came back at all."

Unlike the emotional Tracey Gregor before him, Tony Mullis told his story in a deadpan monotone. As he spoke, the room was stone-silent.

Tony said he had enlisted in the marines out of high school and planned to make the corps his career. Now he had to go in another direction. And though he was not quite certain where that would ultimately take him, it would definitely involve the outdoors. Right now, he told us, he was looking into opening a hunting and fishing camp for men and women like himself who had lost limbs either in combat or in accidents. The one thing he knew, he added, was that his new life would not be complete without the aid of a Service Dog.

"Jeannie and Cason have been a big part of my recovery," he said. "I would not be standing here today if it wasn't for them. But I need my own time, too. I do a lot more physical things than Jeannie ever will, and, y'know, I need that buddy there with me all the time. The rest of my buddies, my human buddies, well, they're either all still in the service or working or off to college. But I am not standing before you here today to tell you I need a hunting dog. What I need is a hunting *buddy,* somebody who's going to be there to watch my back.

"Somebody, I guess, to make me feel . . . " Tony hesitated, the words stuck in his throat, the combat-hardened leatherneck forced in public to admit his greatest fear.

"Safe," he finally said. "Somebody to make me feel safe."

It was as if he had lowered his emotional shield, and I wondered how far he would be able to go with it. Kyria had told me that veterans in general, but especially marines and Special Forces, were p4p's most emotionally problematic clients. When they applied for an Assistance Dog, most had no problem admitting that they needed physical help. A dropped cell phone retrieved, a door opened, a light switch turned on. But companionship to salve damaged psyches? That goes against everything they'd been trained for.

To that end, she said, many of the vets who reach out to p4p, especially those suffering from severe cases of PTSD, are unwilling to face the truth about themselves. At first this bothered Kyria. Until, as she put it, "we found that during the screening process, when they are faced with not receiving a dog if they don't open up to us, even the least-accepting veterans usually own up to their emotional vulnerability."

The organization had once shied away from allowing these veterans into the program. They would not follow the p4p protocols. They were unreliable. They missed veterinarian appointments. They did not groom their dogs properly. And then, when they were dropped from the program, everyone felt as if their time had been wasted. But Terry had pushed for their inclusion. The irony that the man who cannot open up about his own past had gone the extra mile for these troubled veterans was not lost on me.

At any rate, now, Kyria said, "Our doors are open to all. They might not finish, but we're gonna let them start."

Tony Mullis made me aware that some of my own alleged *toughness* had been a facade. It was my habit to return, say, from a war zone closed like a clam. I rarely spoke to anyone, even my wife and son, especially my wife and son, about my experiences. But since I had become involved with paws4people, friends and family told me I seemed changed. My wife, naturally, picked up on it first. Now I could confess to her how frightened I'd been. Or how disgusted or sad or hurt. Laid out in detail. It was a relief, I found, to finally talk to someone who loved and trusted me about the horrors I had witnessed.

This was all going through my mind when Tony Mullis interrupted my reverie. "I guess my biggest problem is, I still worry," he told the crowd.

"At night I lay in bed and I stay up 'til three, four o'clock in the morning just because I worry about somebody comin' through the house and I don't have my legs on. In the marines, I was so used to having that security while I slept, and I don't have that anymore. I've always been the security for my family. But now I gotta say, who's gonna watch out for me, you know?

"And I guess that's the main reason I contacted paws4people. I know there are a lot of guys out there with problems a lot worse than mine. And as hard as it is for me to admit it in front of y'all, I need a lot of things. My wife has to remind me to take my medicine, for instance, and I have to keep a pretty good calendar for my doctors' appointments or I'd totally forget about them. Hell, as it is, I've missed maybe four or five VA appointments since I've been home."

Then Tony turned to address the inmates directly. "Everybody's got that family member that ends up in places like this," he said. "I have one that can't stay out of 'em. But at least you're all doing something to help me, and it means a lot to me. And I thank you very much for everything.

"I guess what I'm trying to say is that it means a lot to me to actually bc here, to be able to tell you my story and for you to be able to respond to it. So I'm real glad we're here to be part of this process. I thank y'all for what you do. And that's all I got to say about it."

The applause for Tony was subdued yet heartfelt. His demeanor, his hesitant speech, his anguish called to mind the plight of the injured veteran Mike Branck, the soft-spoken former air force major whom Allison Kaminsky had introduced to me back in Virginia when she had recertified his Service Dog at the Home Depot. Fallon was the dog's name, a stately Golden Retriever who had passed his tests with flying colors.

Though Tony and Mike came from vastly different backgrounds (before he suffered two traumatic brain injuries while deployed overseas, Mike had earned his BS in environmental engineering, his master's in aerospace science and management, and his PhD in environmental health and safety regulatory affairs), they experienced mutual longings for a *normality* that had been stolen from them in combat. Their reactions were eerily similar.

"This disease has taken its toll in two distinct ways," Mike had told me that day. "Not only in my inability to function but, perhaps worse, in my inability to fulfill my responsibilities as a husband, as a father, as a professional."

As a husband. As a father. I thought of Terry as I watched Tony rejoin Jeannie and Cason. Jeannie hugged him. His boy was still too young to understand what he had just witnessed. He smiled at his daddy and pointed to the dogs lying beneath the inmates' chairs. He wanted to play with them.

Of p4p's more than three hundred clients, a handful, mostly veterans and law enforcement types, have opted to remain anonymous to all but Terry, Kyria, and their closest associates, such as Miami and CeCe. Some of these "confidential clients," as the organization refers to them, are simply ultraprivate individuals. Others are reluctant to disclose their diagnoses for fear of employment discrimination. Yes, that is illegal. It is also a reality.

Mary Dowd is one of those confidential clients, which is why her name and her son's and the Service Dog's with whom she would Bump are the only ones I have changed in this narrative. For as I watched Tony's little Cason point to those dogs, out of the corner of my eye, I saw Mary pick up her cane and limp to the center of the room with what looked to be a painful effort. Then she pulled herself up straight and tall, gripped the podium with both hands, and began to recount her life story.

She spoke about her athletic childhood and of vying for the title of Hawaii's Miss Fitness while earning two bachelor degrees. After college, she joined a police department, she said, and told us about her undercover investigative work and her decision to join the army. It was her demeanor that buckled my knees.

I had seen photos of Mary, who now lived in Virginia, on her p4p application form. She was indeed trim, athletic, and cute in a young Sandra Bullock kind of way. Now, in her midforties, she was the poster woman for traumatic brain injury, standing before us a proud single mother slightly bent, certainly self-conscious, but far from broken. Even her speech wobbled. The words "very athletic" came out *werry at-a-let-ic.*

"I'm sorry about the way I talk," she said and looked to her son, Paul, sitting next to Terry at one of the back tables.

"I have traumatic brain injury, which has messed up my speech neurons." A single tear rolled down her cheek.

When she arrived at army boot camp, she sensed that the male troops resented her gung-ho attitude. They didn't like a woman finishing the obstacle course ahead of them or disassembling, cleaning, and reassembling her rifle faster or doing more situps and pullups. And then bragging about it. "Hoo-Rah Hawaii" they'd called her behind her back. Sometimes to her face.

Then one night the verbal assaults turned physical. A group of fellow soldiers—Mary thinks there were three—all male, their faces obscured behind black balaclavas, cornered her alone in a warehouse. They attacked her with fists and boots and with such a viciousness that she spent, as she remembered with military precision, "two years, nine months, and five days relearning to walk and talk."

There were suspects, but no evidence or confessions. No one was ever charged. Something was fishy. April Cook crossed my mind.

Did the attackers sexually molest Mary? She would not say, not even to Terry and Kyria. That had nearly scotched her application. But then, during her second interview, Terry had a change of heart. If anyone ever needed an Assistance Dog, he felt, it was this woman. Kyria still had her doubts. She expected all p4p's clients to be totally open and honest. Terry pressed. Just this once? We might be saving a life. Kyria relented.

Now, today, here in Hazelton Penitentiary, Mary continued. "My arm was in a sling for over two years," she said, and began to cry softly. "I still cannot wave it over my head without pain. I wear a back brace. Besides the cane, I have two wheelchairs. I can go without using the chair unless I have a stressful day on my feet.

"The time after is the worst part," she said. "It has been well over a decade, but when you are assaulted, sometimes you don't ever heal. When I'm stressed, I suffer from what are called pseudoseizures. They're like epileptic fits, except I'm not an epileptic. I have migraines. I also have PTSD. I do not sleep well. Matter of fact, I haven't slept too well in a couple of days. Coming here, knowing that I had to tell my story in front of you all, just brought up a lot of anxiety.

"You might think I've been standoffish sitting there in the back of the room all by myself. Trust me, I'm not a rude person. I just get real nervous. I know my speech is messed up. It's embarrassing. It's messed up relationships. It's messed up a lot of my life."

For her children, she meant. Her husband had left her, left Mary and their son and an older daughter to fend for themselves on a monthly VA disability check. Now her daughter was grown and gone; she had moved out of the house and was too embarrassed to bring friends around for a visit.

"I understand," Mary said. "She has been pushing me around in a wheelchair since she was ten. My son has had to do the same thing while suffering from ADHD. Yes, the worst part is my children, who have had to suffer through this with me."

Mary's voice, already strained and distorted by her tears, cracked again and again. She dabbed at her cheeks and wiped her glasses dry with the same tissue.

"I feel like part of me has jeopardized my kids' lives because of what they have had to go through. They have seen me on the floor having a seizure. That is so hard for me. I thank God—I really thank God—that I have never had one in public. I don't think I could handle that. I would probably never go out again.

"So receiving a dog gives me hope that my children will be able to lead a more normal life. I try to be a good mother. I really do. I just hope that getting a Service Dog will make me a better mother. A better mother than the one whose disabilities have been holding her back. It's hard. I hurt all over, all the time. My knees. My spine. My neck. Sometimes I feel like they are beating me all over again. And that thought brings on the migraines and the seizures."

Mary ran off a laundry list of medical diagnoses—arthritis, bursitis, fibromyalgia, neurological damage, degenerative joint disease, spine deterioration—and when she was finished, she paused to again meet her son's gaze. She lifted the soggy and torn tissue to her face, and I noticed Terry slip a handkerchief from his pocket, hand it to Paul, and point him to his mother. He ran to her side and hugged her.

With her damaged arm draped over her son's shoulders, Mary extended the other to encompass the inmate trainers, the paws4people volunteers, the other clients and their families, the prison staff. Her hand trembled with the effort.

I did not think that she would be able to continue.

But then she said, "I just want to thank you all for your time and for your help and for your prayers. I want to thank you from the bottom of my heart for all your hard work. You, all of you, are a blessing for people like me."

And then Mary Dowd took a deep breath, stood erect, and retrieved her cane. With Paul by her side, she walked slowly to her seat. The room erupted in a standing ovation.

Chapter Eight

The Bump (2)

The long night is over. Puppy number eight, another girl, arrives at 4:29 a.m.

At 14.08 ounces, the soon-to-be-named Darby—the US Army's Camp Darby is in Livorno, Italy—is the second lightest of the litter, outweighing Shelby by 0.03 pound. Terry hands me the snipped and clipped tiny ball of fur, and I festoon her with a length of purple yarn. By now I'm an old hand at this tying-off stuff, even starting to enjoy it. It makes me feel useful, and I'm a little sad that Darby's arrival will end my contributions.

Claire—panting, exhausted, tongue lolling—has collapsed in a heap on her birthing bed, looking like a pile of rumpled laundry. But all eight pups appear healthy, happy, and hungry. As I watch the six boys and two girls tumble over each other maneuvering for positions at her teats, my mind yet again wanders into the future. Where will these dogs be in two years? What shattered lives will they help piece back together? Who will they *choose*?

It was Kyria who first came up with the notion of allowing the dogs to "select their own humans." Now, as she crawls along the floor and uses her arms as a wedge to clear room for Darby and

Shelby at Claire's belly—the boys are crowding them out—she explains that the idea came to her at the organization's first Bump, in 2008. She was still a junior in college, and p4p's first two clients, both young girls, were the only participants. At the time, the prison program was still in its infancy—Hazelton was its only facility—and it had but a handful of dogs in training.

One of those girls, a preteen named Grace, was a quadriplegic confined to a motorized wheelchair. But it was the other, the ten-year-old Amanda, whom Kyria recalls with a particular nostalgia. She was the first client p4p ever Bumped. Amanda suffered from brain damage that induced periodic seizures. Her syndrome impaired her motor skills, and she wore braces on both legs and required a walker. She was also afflicted with an immune deficiency disorder, and her parents covered her face with a surgical mask when she was out in public.

"I was worried about the equipment," Kyria remembers. "How the dogs would react to Grace's power chair and Amanda's walker and braces, even her mask. It meant they would not be able to read her facial expressions. We knew that these girls were not the, quote-unquote, typical humans that the dogs had interacted with in the prison."

That first Bump occurred a year before Kyria would journey to California's Sonoma Valley to study at Bonnie Bergin's University of Canine Studies. But an experienced volunteer trainer working with p4p had graduated from the Bergin program, and she described for Kyria and Terry how the Bergin matchmaking system worked. It tapped into what evolutionary biologists call the study of animalities—that is, the accumulation of evidence from a wide variety of species, but dogs in particular, that suggests that certain animals are not part of a monolithic animal kingdom acting in concert but instead demonstrate consistent differences in their behavior. These differences often map directly onto the sorts of patterns we see in human personalities—shyness, for instance, or risk taking.

Using this research, the Bergin administrators had honed a placement process wherein applicants for Assistance Dogs were asked to complete extensive written personality profiles about themselves. They were then paired with dogs whose temperaments the school felt best matched up with their psychological and emotional histories.

"Pretty much straight bio stuff," Kyria says. "Likes and dislikes. Placing amiable to amiable, reliable to reliable, outgoing to outgoing, attention-needing to attention-needing."

Yet something bothered Kyria about the cut-and-dried nature of the Bergin process. She instinctively sensed that such "straight matchups" would not suit what she and Terry had in mind for their clients. What was the answer? Good question. This was all virgin territory. But she had some thoughts. For one, she says, she planned on bringing all of p4p's dogs into the Bump, one at a time, to meet each client individually.

As she tells me a story, she picks up Darby, shakes her head, and lets out a small laugh. "That first time, it just seemed like the sensible thing to do."

There were only three dogs ready to be placed with clients in 2008, and Kyria had them meet Amanda first, then Grace. The Bergin system's by-the-book matchups, the personality profiles, were a guideline. But more important was how each dog would interact with, and react to, the girls.

"Ellie is the dog's name who Bumped with Amanda, and Ellie was just glued to her from the moment they met. When the other dogs were led out, they needed to check out her leg braces and walker. They seemed to have trepidations, and they were a little suspicious of her mask. But Ellie just bounded up to Amanda and did not want to leave her. When the inmate handler took Ellie away, she just kept looking back, and every time she got some slack in her leash, she bolted back toward Amanda. It was a really obvious first Bump; Ellie wanted Amanda. And it kind of set the precedent. It worked that time, and it's worked at every Bump since.

"My goodness," she says. "Now that I remember it, we didn't even call them Bumps back then."

In fact, it was Terry who came up with the term; as he watched Amanda and Ellie interact, he turned to Kyria and said, "They just bumped into each other, and already they're in love."

They have been using the term ever since.

Of course, Kyria adds, the real key to the success of p4p's placement system, the revolutionary concept that places the organization apart from other Assistance Dog providers, is the innovation that she and Terry devised wherein the Bump is merely the prelude to the matching process. Kyria admits that she does not pay much attention to rival organizations. Even if she did, she says, "Most don't really like to say much about the way they work. Barring interviewing a client who has gone through another organization's matching process—which I have not—it's kind of hard to know about the intricacies of what they do.

"But what I do know is that most will just tell the clients to come in and they'll match each with one dog. Some, like Bonnie Bergin's, do the research. Some don't. I've seen documentaries about organizations who say they let the dogs pick the people. But then you watch them just letting all the dogs out into a room with all the clients at the same time. It's kind of like, well, wherever the dogs end up is who they *pick*. The client maybe trains with the dog for ten days, and that's it.

"So I think the radical part of what we do is not only how

young our dogs are when they select their humans but how early in the dog's training process we match them with clients at Bumps. Sometimes it's almost a year before we let them go home together because we spend that intervening time customizing the dog to the client's special needs. That is where we're really different. I've never heard of anyone else who does that."

Now, with five years of placements under her belt, Kyria concedes that the Bergin matchup policy generally works best with children and juveniles. Their parents, after all, are primarily seeking physical companions for their kids—dogs to pull their wheelchairs and pick up dropped items. Would Amanda and Ellie have worked so well (the two are still together), would any of the p4p placements have worked so well, had Kyria gone strictly by a personality profile? Possibly. But according to the p4p dossiers on the other dogs at that first Bump, for instance, they also matched up well with Amanda.

Thus there is no substitute, she says, for the eyeball test, particularly when it comes to placing Assistance Dogs with combat veterans like April Cook and Tony Mullis, women and men in need of psychological Service Dogs. More often than not, these veterans function at a higher level when they are paired with dogs "with polar-opposite temperaments."

"Granted," she says, "this isn't a hard-and-fast rule. Personalities aren't fixed for entire lives, people change. Look at April, how far she's come. But in general we've seen that if you match a vet who is shy or skittish or brooding—and they're our bread and butter, so to speak—with a dog who shows similar traits, the two of them would end up holed up in their room forever.

"So with vets we often go—often, not always—with an opposites-attract theory. Of course, when I say *we*, I'm talking about the dogs. It's their Bump."

As Kyria speaks, I notice that she constantly, if subconsciously, picks up a different puppy to stroke and coo in its ear before placing it back in the scrum vying for Claire's milk. The students look on with envy. As for the Bumps themselves, she says their contours have been refined over the years, the rough corners sanded.

The first few, she remembers, were a little more "mobby" than today's orderly procedures. "Everyone was out in the room, milling around while we brought the dogs in one at a time," she says.

"There wasn't as much formality as now. It took some time to decide what kind of rooms we like to be in, for example, and how far away everyone observing should sit. You know, you don't want to distract the dogs while they're being introduced to the client. On the other hand, they *are* going to be out in public with them, so having people around during a Bump kind of helps to set a tone. Another thing we changed was with the inmate handlers. In the beginning, they stayed in the room when the dogs met the clients. Now they don't.

"The Bumps have evolved in that sense," she says. "But the general idea remains the same."

I mention that it strikes me that there is almost something, well, *mystical* about the p4p matching process; that in order to get it right, Kyria and Terry must have had to develop some kind of mysterious insight that requires not only a keen mind and open heart but also a deep curiosity about the ways of the human spirit.

Kyria chuckles at this. "I don't know if I'd put it that way," she says. "But there is a large subjective component. Where my dad and I just *get* what we're seeing, what we're looking for, what we want.

"But there's a major scientific aspect, too. You have to be able to analyze the body language cues. Which is why I guess the smartest change I've made since the early Bumps was to decide to sit right there, next to the clients."

"To read their body language?" I ask.

"No, silly. The dogs'."

—————————————————

We broke for lunch early, at just past 11:00. I noticed that a few of the clients were too nervous to eat the generous buffet prepared by Hazelton's inmate kitchen staff. Mary Dowd barely picked at her food, while the heaping plate Jeannie Mullis had prepared for Tony remained untouched. I also passed on the meal in order to step outside with two male corrections officers taking a smoke break.

By now the snow was more blowing than falling, but the temperature still hovered in the low teens, and the afternoon sky had taken on the macabre formality of a steel engraving. The two guards—tall and short; skinny and, well, not so skinny—threw off a kind of Mutt-and-Jeff aura, and as we shivered near the front gate, I asked straight off what they thought of the prison dog program.

The tall guard surprised me. He said how impressed he was by the way the p4p program allowed the inmates "to begin shaping their postprison lives." Conditioned by watching years of prison movies, I was not expecting such a sensitive answer from a "screw."

"Most of these women get out and, well, they'll be right back inside for something 'cause they're not prepared," the tall guard continued. "The inmates who work with the dogs, at least they're learning a trade, even if it's just dog grooming. And it's not so easy on them in here. Some of the other inmates, the hard cases, they try to make life tough. Call 'em 'brownnosers.' Pretend that they're allergic to the dogs or just plain scared of them. Anything to get under the handlers' skin. It's their way of picking on them. And I've got a lot of admiration for the gals who stick it out through that kind of intimidation."

His partner, the shorter guard, had a cantilevered face and a thin, wispy beard that hung from his chin like Spanish moss. He was less sanguine than his partner and shrugged as if to convey the sentiment, *Such is life in a federal prison.* Then he added, "Most of these women are lost causes. Trying to rehabilitate them is like trying to plant cut flowers. But I will say this for the program. From our point of view, the more of them busy training dogs, the less trouble they can get into. You know, idle hands and all that."

At that moment a third guard poked her head out the door. "They're starting up again," she said.

Back inside, I counted seven dogs lined up in the corridor outside the dining hall. Terry moved among the handlers, making last-minute arrangements about the order in which they would appear. I waited for him. He was preoccupied. But I had to ask.

"Terry, tell me the truth. You ever get a gut feeling before one of these Bumps about which dog is going to choose which client?"

"No," he said. "I intentionally try not to."

"Because you don't want to be disappointed?" I asked.

"Nah. I've learned from experience that it's a waste of my time because I'm usually wrong. It's one of those things that just sort of happens the way it happens. To this day I don't understand how the dogs do what they do. We joke about it all the time. It's like they go back into the back room after they meet the clients for the first time and say, 'I want this one; you take that one.' Then they come out the second time and that's who they get."

He paused, still eyeing the row of animals. "It's hard to explain until you see it with your own eyes. We've been doing this a long time, and you just kind of *know* when they click."

Back inside the dining hall, the food had been put away; the paper plates and cups had been bussed from the tables where the p4p contingent of clients, students, and visitors sat, and the podium in the middle of the room had been removed. Perhaps a third of the inmates—the lead trainers—were out in the hallway with their dogs. The rest remained seated in rows, the dogs in training still resting at their feet.

Four metal folding chairs had been moved to a corner in the front of the large hall. Josh Gregor and his parents, Tracey and Brian, occupied three of them. Kyria sat in the fourth, just a little removed. There was maybe twenty feet of open space between Kyria, the Gregors, and the rest of us. Terry, Chaeney at his side, stood all the way in the back of the hall. His vantage point allowed him to make eye contact with Kyria as well as the head inmate trainer on the other side of the room. The head inmate trainer held a steno pad in her lap.

Terry had told me a little of what to expect. As the clients interacted with the dogs, Kyria and he would communicate through a long-practiced series of subtle head nods, shrugs, eye contact, raised eyebrows, and other (human) body language cues. Terry generally followed Kyria's lead, and when they had reached a silent agreement, he would then wordlessly flash "scores" with his fingers, between one and ten, to the head inmate trainer. She would put the number down next to each dog's name. The higher the score, the more compatibility they sensed between dog and client. I moved into a position to peer over the trainer's shoulder as the dogs were led in by the handlers one at a time.

Common sense dictated that there be some limitations to the pairings. The eighty-pound chocolate Labrador Jock, whom I had met here at Hazelton two months earlier, for instance, was not yet ready to be Bumped. But had he been, Terry and Kyria would certainly have been hesitant to present such a large, imposing animal to frail, little Josh Gregor. The opposite was generally true of large soldiers or veterans and smallish dogs. That said, we had a nice mix today.

The Golden Retriever Avery was led out first. His handler took him a few feet into the hall, unhooked his leash from his collar, and backed out of the room. Avery immediately drew back as if overwhelmed by the one hundred or so people focused on him. His eyes darted about the hall, and he sat back on his haunches with his tail between his legs. Kyria frowned.

There is an entire science devoted to the study of dog body language, and Kyria has mastered the nuances of the hundreds of subsets of calming signals and distance-increasing signals and stress signals and stress vocalizations and marking signals and displacement behaviors. These range—to name but a very few—from "pacing" to "bunny eyes" to "cheek puffing" to "yawning" to "whale eyes" to "stretching" to, my favorite, the "muzzle punch," wherein an agitated dog jumps up and clocks you in the jaw or nose.

"It's how they communicate," Kyria had explained to me. "And if you know how to read those cues, you'll see the difference between 'I want you to stay close to me and give me affection' and 'I'm only here because I know I'm supposed to be standing right here.'

"Take their ears. Our breeds, Goldens and Labs, they can't point them straight to the sky. But they can definitely lift them, which means 'alert.' They can pin them backward, flip them almost so that they're inside out—it's called bunny ears—and that usually means 'stress.' If they're just hanging down naturally, it means the dog is comfortable."

Some body language cues, like Avery's tucked tail, are obvious to the average person as a classic fear response. Others are more subtle, if not altogether invisible or even the opposite of what we think. Contrary to what we commonly assume, for instance, Kyria told me that "a wagging tail means nothing on its face. A dog can wag its tail because it's about to bite you, or a dog can wag its tail because it's happy and content. You have to know how to read the difference."

At this moment, Avery appeared far from happy and content. When Josh extended his arm to pet him, the dog visibly flinched. Kyria walked over and half-pulled, half-carried him closer to the Gregors, and all three took turns petting his scruff, rubbing his ears, and addressing him in baby-doggy talk. Avery showed little response. After five or six minutes, Josh seemed to give up, although Tracey and Brian carried on gamely. Terry's eyes met Kyria's. She shook her head imperceptibly. Terry nodded and made a subtle *o* with his thumb and index finger. The scorekeeper wrote a "0" next to Avery's name.

Next into the hall came Harper, the white Labradoodle who had so charmed me on my earlier visit to Hazelton. Harper also appeared intimidated by the surroundings and circumstances and paid Josh barely more attention than Avery had. Terry signaled another "0."

Madison, a chocolate Labrador and a shelter rescue dog, arrived next. Finally, some interaction between dog and humans. Josh flashed a broad grin as he gently ran his hands along Madison's back and tickled her chin. Madison licked his hand in appreciation. Then the dog carefully moved closer to Josh and licked his face gently. Josh grinned like a jack-o'-lantern.

When Madison stepped toward Tracey and Brian, they both stroked her with enthusiasm. The three clients played this way with Madison for a good fifteen to twenty minutes as a few people in the room "oohed" and "aahed." Terry took his cue from Kyria and held both of his hands close to his chest. Five fingers were extended on one, three on the other. The trainer wrote "8" next to Madison's name.

Madison had barely departed before the Golden Retriever Frances pranced into the dining hall, beelined for Josh, and extended her paw. After several moments of Josh's vigorous petting, the dog stretched out on the floor, rolled over, and allowed all three Gregors to rub her belly.

I watched keenly as Frances hit the floor. From the little I knew—that is, from what Kyria had taught me—a dog's belly-up pose can signal two distinct reactions. If it performs an easy, shoulder-rolling, butt-flipping descent to the ground—"goofy and wiggly," Kyria called it—this is attention-seeking behavior. The dog is happy and is asking for a belly rub. On the other hand, if it rapidly flings itself to the ground, rolls belly-up, and tucks its tail, this is a signal that it wants to get away. This latter is called a tap out—akin to a wrestling tap out—and it means, "Stop touching me."

Frances had prostrated herself before Josh in the "wiggly and goofy" style, and as the boy fell to his knees beside her, he flashed the same thousand-watt smile. Frances quite obviously also loved this, and her tail wagged back and forth like a metronome on speed. No one watching could miss the connection between this dog and Josh and his family. On Terry's signal, the scorekeeper wrote "10."

Frances was reluctant to be led away—I would have ended the proceedings right there—but it was time to make way for Sampson, a big yellow Lab. Sampson was as friendly as Frances, though I thought him much too large for Josh. The dog looked as if he might swallow the boy whole as he showered his face with licks. Josh, however, loved the affection, and boy giggled and dog woofed as Sampson lay down before Josh for his turn of belly rubs. This time Terry made a more elaborate series of signals and the scorekeeper marked Sampson's appearance with an "8/9."

The Golden Retriever Morgan came next, and again I remembered her from my earlier visit. Morgan showed the most curiosity about the tubes flowing from Josh's backpack to under his shirt. After basking in Josh's pets for a few minutes, she walked a complete circle around the boy, pausing for several long moments to ponder and sniff the tubes. She then returned to the front and laid her head in Josh's lap. Every shoulder in the room sagged with emotion. Morgan played with Josh and his parents for a good long while before Terry and Kyria exchanged glances. Terry gave Morgan an "8."

The final entry was Noel, another Golden Retriever. Noel was smallish for a Golden, and the poor, shivering dog looked as frightened as Avery and Harper to take center stage before so many strangers. Again Kyria left her seat and tried to coax Noel into playing with Josh and his parents. She cajoled him into a position to be petted by all three, and though the affection seemed to relax Noel a bit, she kept her head on a swivel, eyeing the crowd as often as the Gregors. It took only a few moments for Kyria to mercifully signal Noel's handler that she had seen enough.

Kyria looked at Terry. Her shoulders shrugged. Terry extended three fingers across his chest. I supposed it was for just showing up, like a gentleman's C.

And so, at just under 90 minutes, ended Josh's first round. The initial encounter between clients and dogs serves as a getting-to-know-you introduction for both. The nonresponsive animals would be eliminated, and I guessed that Madison the chocolate Lab, Sampson the yellow Lab, and the two Golden Retrievers, Frances and Morgan, would make the cut to Josh's second round.

Next up was Tony Mullis, who paused to whisper something into Josh Gregor's ear as they passed in the center of the dining hall. I don't know what he said, but the boy's grin gave me a pretty good idea. (Later, Tony told me he'd said that the marines could use a few good men like Josh.) Meanwhile, Terry and Kyria took a few minutes to confer and decided to remove Noel from the rest of the day's Bumps. "Needs more seasoning," Terry said.

Tony underwent Round One alone—Jeannie and Cason would join him for Round Two—and as he settled into the "hot seat" near Kyria, he still struck me as somewhat uncomfortable being the center of attention. He pawed at the floor with his New Balances, like a nervous thoroughbred at the starting gate; shoved his hands into the pockets of his cargo shorts; took them out and wrung them together; and shoved them back in again. It suddenly dawned on me—what if none of the dogs "chose" Tony? I wondered if he was having the same thoughts.

The dogs would not necessarily meet Tony—or Mary, for that matter—in the same order in which they had come to Josh. But as it happened, Avery was again first up, and again it was immediately apparent that there was no compatibility. The Golden Retriever backed away from Tony's prosthetic legs as if repelled by some invisible force field, and Terry made the familiar sign with his thumb and index finger. The head trainer wrote "0."

Harper was next, and she looked to have shaken off the stage fright she exhibited with Josh. Harper nuzzled Tony while the former marine ran his hands through her scruff. The two got on well, but for the life of me, I could not envision this cute, white, fluffy Labradoodle at Tony's side on hunting and fishing trips into the

Georgia backcountry. Apparently neither could Terry or Kyria. The head trainer marked "4/5" next to Harper's name.

Then Madison loped into the room, and Tony's wide-eyed face lit up at the sight of the big chocolate Lab. Tony started off with strong pets that morphed into great bear hugs, and the two seemed to forget there was anyone else in the room as Tony eased himself from the chair. He sat on the floor next to the rugged dog, threw his arms around her, and the two veritably wrestled for a good fifteen minutes.

Toward the end, when Tony sat back in his chair, Madison turned and scooted her butt in between his prostheses. This, I knew, was "claiming behavior," a signal that she wanted a butt scratch. This surprised me. It generally means that the dog is truly comfortable and happy with the human and wants to be with him. Kyria had told me that this does not usually occur until the second round. In any case, I felt that this was the kind of Assistance Dog a legless marine could feel safe with either at home at night or out in the piney woods. Why Terry signaled a mere "8/9" and not a "10," I had no idea.

Frances was next, and though I saw little chemistry between her and Tony—the petting seemed formulaic and perfunctory—she was given a "7." But when Sampson followed her in, I suspected that if Madison was going to have any competition for Tony's affections, it would come from this big yellow Labrador. Like Madison, Sampson just looked the part of the "buddy" Tony said he needed. Tony again slid off of his chair to roughhouse on the floor, and when it was time for Sampson to depart, Tony glanced at Kyria with a look every parent has seen from a child at bedtime. *Just five more minutes. Please.* Everyone in the room, quiet as a library until then, let out a soft "awww."

Kyria smiled and waved off Sampson's trainer. Tony grabbed

the dog's head with both hands, scratched his ears, and then pulled him close to his own face and rubbed noses with him. Kyria was still grinning as the scorekeeper glanced at Terry and noted a "9" next to Sampson's name, giving him the slightest edge on Madison. Morgan's subsequent appearance—and her score of "8"—struck me as anticlimactic.

It was a two-dog race for Tony between Madison and Sampson, and everyone in the room sensed it.

By the time Mary took her seat, I felt as if I was getting a handle on the human-dog connections Terry and Kyria were seeing. Like Tony's Jeannie and Cason, Paul would join his mother for Round Two, but for now it was Mary very much alone in the front of that room. She looked so fragile that I was afraid one of the larger dogs might bowl her over, and I turned to catch Paul shoot her a thumbs-up from his table in the back.

It was a further letdown when—yet again—poor Avery exhibited no compatibility whatsoever with Mary. Even with Kyria prodding the Golden Retriever, Avery still seemed more interested in the crowd than in the client. I guessed it was just not Avery's day. Terry gave her a third straight "0."

Harper, however, nearly jumped up onto Mary's lap and showered her with kisses the moment her handler dropped the leash. Mary's face creased into a smile that widened and brightened as she wrapped both her arms around the pretty white Labradoodle. At one point I followed her gaze across the room to Paul, who reacted with a beatific smile of his own. Folks, I thought, we have a winner. Terry backed me up by flashing a "9" to the scorekeeper. But yet again I had reacted too soon.

For although Madison proved much too big and boundy for Mary and Morgan made a respectable showing, earning a score of "6," it was Frances and Sampson who made late runs for

Mary's affection. Sampson was the bigger surprise by far. Because of his size, I was certain that he, too, would overwhelm Mary. But the two hit it off from Mary's first stroke of his scruff, and within moments they were hugging and snuggling. Sampson earned a "9."

Yet it was Frances who again took center stage. It was as if the Golden Retriever had studied the Labradoodle Harper's performance and was trying to top it. She inched onto Mary's lap, showered her with kisses, and even sniffed and laid her head against her wounded arm. The compatibility between the two was palpable, and Frances walked away with her second "10" of the afternoon. If you threw in the "7" Frances earned with Tony, it was as if she had decided she wanted all three of the clients to take her home. Maybe she was just that sick of prison life.

A twenty-minute break between rounds ensued, and I tablehopped as inconspicuously as possible to eavesdrop. The Gregors were over the moon; everything they had been told to expect from a Bump had occurred. Tracey and Brian debated the merits of each dog while Josh whispered something to his sister Elizabeth. He finally turned to his parents and said, "I told her it doesn't matter which one, I love them all."

A few feet away, Mary was more circumspect; I suspected circumspection was her default mode. She and Paul held hands, although neither said much. At one point Terry approached her and gently massaged her shoulders from behind. She turned and looked up at him and smiled. "It's going really well," he said. "You and your son ready to get up there?" Mary nodded. Her smile appeared to grow.

Meanwhile, Tony had taken Cason in his arms as Jeannie went to find coffee. He cooed to his little boy that they'd soon be bringing home a dog. "Do you want to meet a doggie? Would you like to live with a doggie?"

Cason pointed toward the side door where the dogs entered. "That's right, son," Tony said. "Now we're gonna meet some doggies together. You, me, and Mommy. You like that?" Cason kissed his father's forehead.

With Noel dismissed altogether, Josh's field was narrowed to four dogs on his second trip to the "hot seat." What a difference a half hour made. Frances, who just hours before had earned her first "10" cavorting with Josh, now barely acknowledged his presence. She was completely indifferent to the young boy's pleas to play with him, and she was led away within minutes. Terry scored her a "0," and I remembered his remarks about the dogs secretly meeting in the hallway between rounds to divvy up clients. It was as if Frances realized she could not have all three and had set her sights on someone else.

Not so with Sampson. Once again, the big yellow Lab practically flew into Josh's arms. Tracey and Brian Gregor had been joined for this round by Elizabeth, and though the entire family embraced Sampson, I remembered Josh telling us this morning that he was looking forward to being paired with a Golden Retriever. Nonetheless, Sampson earned an "8." He was not going down without a fight.

Morgan seemed to sense this. Now that it was her turn, the exuberant Golden Retriever exhibited the same curiosity as she had earlier toward the tube apparatus that ran from Josh's backpack. Despite her obvious excitement, there was a certain gentility to the dog's approach as she seemed to take the time to figure out where Josh was injured or hurt and zero in on that spot.

She licked Josh's ears instead of his entire face, for instance, and though Sampson had been just as affectionate, I got the feeling that the emotional connection between Morgan and Josh ran deeper. It was, I suppose, Morgan's sensitivity to Josh's impairments that put the dog over the top for me. The way she sniffed at the tubes. The way she concentrated on Josh's hearing aid. Kyria let the two play for a good twenty minutes. Although Elizabeth got in a few pets toward the end of the session, Tracey and Brian left the stage to their son and what I was certain was his new Assistance Dog.

Kyria barely flicked her chin toward Terry, who signaled the scorekeeper. She wrote "9" next to Morgan's name. Madison was waiting in the wings, but after another glance from Kyria, Terry indicated to the chocolate Lab's inmate handler that the dog need not even bother entering the room. It was all but officially over. I was betting that Josh would indeed receive his Golden Retriever.

Terry and Kyria broke up the human order of appearance for the second round—"Just a whim," Kyria told me—and Mary took her seat with Paul by her side. The transformation was startling. Mary looked like a different person. Gone was the wobbly woman with the slumped shoulders and tentative, halting carriage. In her place there appeared a much more confident and poised person. She looked stronger physically, sitting straight in her chair with just a hint of a smile, and even the lines in her face had softened. Then it hit me. Mary had walked across the room without her cane. It was as if meeting the dogs in Round One, perhaps combined with her cathartic speech, had broken an emotional dam.

Terry and Kyria had winnowed Mary's second round to three dogs, and when Harper bounded out first, it was impossible to miss the same connection the Labradoodle had exhibited earlier with Mary. Even the twelve-year-old Paul felt it; the three cuddled and played together for close to twenty minutes. I suspected this was a fait accompli, yet for some reason Terry and Kyria saw fit to drop Harper's score with Mary to an "8" from her earlier "9." Not only that, but when Frances followed Harper, she also received an "8." Then Terry, again on a nod from Kyria, waved off Sampson's second meeting with Mary. I suspected they were saving him for Tony and the two-Labrador race for his affections.

There was kind of a prize-fight-night tension in the air as Tony, Jeannie, and Cason took their seats. *Ladies and gentlemen, in one corner, with the chocolate hue, the Labrador Madison. In the opposite corner, in yellow, her opponent the Labrador Sampson.* Alas, the contest lasted for all of a few moments. Tony and Madison had obviously bonded during Round One. You could tell from the joy they took in each other's company. But I think Madison's immediate devotion to Jeannie and Cason, apparent at first glance, abruptly ended the competition. The toddler showed no fear as Madison ran excited circles around him, pausing only to be petted and, in turn, acknowledging Cason's strokes with big, wet kisses.

While the Mullis family played with Madison, Terry crossed the room and whispered something into the lead inmate trainer's ear. She wrote "15" next to Madison's name. Their connection was off the official charts.

I thought that would be it, as did most everyone else in the room. Chairs scraped the linoleum floor and soft conversations started up. The observers were beginning to move to congratulate all three clients when Kyria stood and frantically signaled Terry, still standing beside the scorekeeper.

"Folks, folks, please hold on a sec," he announced. "We just feel we should see one more thing."

At Kyria's nod, Sampson was led into the room. Sampson was good with Tony, Jeannie, and especially Cason, but even he seemed to sense that it was too late. Terry whispered again, and the scorer marked "8½." Then I noticed Morgan being held by a leash near the door, ready to follow Sampson. *No, no,* I thought, *not Josh's Morgan!* But Terry and Kyria shook their heads, and Morgan's handler backed her off.

I had kept my own scorecard—heavily influenced, of course, by the scorekeeper's official tally—and had paired Tony with Madison, Josh with Morgan, and Mary with Harper the cute Labradoodle. But it turned out there had been a rare tie, and Terry and Kyria decided to begin training both Sampson and Morgan for Josh. Weeks down the road, it would turn out, Morgan got the call (as I had predicted). But the real curveball: Kyria and Terry saw a connection between Mary and Frances that I had completely missed.

Later that night, back down the mountain, I invited Terry and Kyria to a late dinner at a Ruby Tuesday across the street from our Morgantown motel. They trudged in and shook the snow from their boots looking satisfied, if exhausted. We'd spent almost nine hours at the prison and another two on the road driving to and from Hazelton. I probed gently for what is referred to in military circles as an after-action report.

Kyria said they felt the Bump had gone "pretty much by the book. No big question marks, no big concerns, no big surprises. Even Avery and Noel—it was their first Bump. Sometimes it takes one, maybe even two, for the dogs to understand the process."

Terry for the most part agreed, though he did allow that Madison's selection of Tony was a mild upset. Shelter dogs like Madison, he said, usually arrive at p4p with a host of anxieties. "Baggage," he called it. Separation issues, aggression issues, sometimes even just a plain old fear of humans. "Probably means they were whipped," he said.

As with p4p's human clients, he added, those anxieties can be triggered by specific, if unexpected, forms. "A big man in a baseball hat. A young female child. Even the color of a T-shirt."

I thought of April and her reaction to uniforms.

"Sometimes," he said, "no matter how hard we try, we can't get them past that baggage. But the ladies at Alderson, from the second or third week of Madison's arrival, they kept telling me that she was going to amount to something. Obviously, she has. I'm happy for her. She's a sweet dog, and she's going to do well in that family."

Then Kyria admitted that she had initially leaned toward the Golden Retriever Morgan as a pairing for Tony, primarily because of "how accepting" the dog was toward his prosthetic legs. But because of the way Tony and Madison played together, she knew the competition was over.

"When they were tussling together, Madison just looked up at Tony, and in that instant she got it. She got it without anyone having to teach her. She was interested, accepting, patient, and gentle around his legs. Then in Round Two, the eye contact she made with Tony and his wife and especially the baby, she was just connecting."

You mean, I asked, Sampson never had a shot?

"Believe it or not," she said, "I felt Sampson almost liked Cason too much. This is Tony's dog, after all. That's what we mean when we say the dog picks its person. When Madison met the family, she wasn't like, 'Oh my God, I'm so glad all of you are here.' It was more like, 'I like all of you, but Tony is my person.' So that one wasn't rocket science."

When talk turned to Josh and his long-suffering parents, Terry's eyes dampened while talking about "the kind of hand Tracey and Brian were dealt."

"I don't know if I'd have the grace or the ability to accept it the way these families do," he said. "It's what their path is, I guess. The battle they fight, it's an inspiration. And that's what we live off of, to tell you the truth. The funny thing is, at each Bump it's almost as if what these families say is coming off the same script they've all read beforehand. But of course they don't even know each other. Yet they all speak about what blessings their kids are, what gifts.

"That's one of the beauties about working with the kids. Josh, Alex Keefover, Emilia. Going all the way back to the special needs classrooms."

He shook his head. "To see that spirit."

Kyria laid her head on her father's shoulder and closed her eyes, and a collage of memories, distant and recent, floated through my head: my visit with Emilia Bartlinski; Alex Keefover's determination in willing himself to become a meteorologist; Jeff Mitchell's wrenching letters from the battlefield; Morgan's attention to Josh Gregor's tubes and hearing aids. It also crossed my mind, not for the first time, that perhaps, on a deeper level, the daughter had thrown herself into paws4people in order to heal the father.

Naturally, this notion had occurred to me before—the irony of Terry making everyone involved with the organization, from inmates to clients, reveal themselves so nakedly while he himself remained so tight-lipped about his own emotional disorder was unavoidable. Once I'd even asked Kyria flat-out if she had gotten into the Assistance Dog business for her father's sake, to provide him with a means of at least coping with his demons (if not vanquishing them). She'd more or less avoided the intent of my question, saying merely that she hoped that paws4people, and its expected growth, would provide a soft physical landing platform for her dad as he grew older.

But I suspected there was more to it than that. In fact, I wouldn't be surprised if she had put her plan in motion to "heal" her father as far back as her childhood, when Riley entered her life and she saw how his presence affected her grandparents.

We ate in silence for a time, alone with our distilled thoughts. As we sat there, Kyria and Terry had been desultorily snatching french fries and onion rings from each other's plates, and I knew the mood had lightened when he fake-slapped her hand and she giggled. Time for one final question about Mary and Frances—how, I wondered, had I gotten it so round-the-bend wrong between Mary and Harper? It must have been something in my voice. They both smiled, and Terry wagged his finger. "You better watch it, Drury. You actually sound like you're starting to care about this stuff instead of just reporting what happens."

Kyria piled on. "Oh, no, Dad, not him. He's too hard for that."

Then she reached over and patted my hand in an exaggerated *there-there* manner. "Don't feel bad," she said. "We talked about converting you a long time ago. We both figured you'd just need time to come around."

I took a long swig of my beer. Was I about to tell them that perhaps the time I'd spent observing paws4people had in fact softened me? No, not softened me. Opened me. So many months ago I'd arrived in Fort Stewart determined to be the first to report the story of how Assistance Dogs were improving suffering veterans' lives. I'd never read or heard that story angle before, and I was guessing neither did my readers. I'd be the first to write it. The improved lives themselves? All well and good, but secondary to the story. And the story was the process.

I'd been a reporter for so long, trying to get the story first, that I'd lost sight of a greater picture. My attitude had been, "Hey, it's war. People die. Some people who don't die return with physical, psychological, and emotional scars. I'm sorry for them, but I have my own friends and family to worry over." Now I cared. And as much as I felt for the vets, I think it was the kids who had somehow *turned* me. I worried over them, over their recoveries, over the quality of their future lives. The kids, who reminded me of my own boy—and how lucky I am.

When Liam-Antoine was less than a year old, his pediatrician informed me and his mother that one of his tear ducts had failed to open properly, and the doctor would have to "clean it out" with a long needle. I was beside myself with fear for the boy, much like I was the time I rushed him to the hospital after he stumbled into a wasps' nest and was stung a half-dozen times. Yet these travails now seemed, well, trivial when compared to those of the child clients of p4p.

All these jumbled thoughts were flashing through my mind when Kyria said, "You asked about Mary and Frances? At every single Bump, no matter what anyone thinks"—and here she glanced at her father—"I make a different decision in at least one of the matches. Maybe one dog will look as if it *likes* a certain person better in a vacuum, but I'm also thinking about the family dynamics, like with Madison and the Mullises.

"So I'm going to sound like such a quack when I say this, but when Frances was with Mary the first time and got in her lap, and they were face-to-face in that moment, it was like everything about Mary's person and her emotions and what she was giving off just changed. A complete shift, as if there were a color around her, and it changed the room from black to blue or purple, to something happy. Everyone saw it the second time, but sitting up there next to them, I *felt* it straight off."

Here Terry interrupted. "If you'll allow me to be a little touchy-feely here," he said. "Remember how I explained that the dogs are like sponges, sucking that negative karma from you? I saw that in Mary today. Suddenly she's got six or seven dogs coming out to meet her, and they're all drawing a little bit of it out of her."

Kyria nodded and said, "Then there was the magnetism to Frances's body language when she cuddled with Mary. Really, I didn't want to break it up. If it weren't for the time constraint, I would have let them stay that way all day."

Kyria further surprised me when she said that, in Mary's case, she considered Harper a distant third to Sampson.

"Mary is very soft and quiet," she said. "So do you want to place her with an opposites-attract dog like Sampson, who's kind of bubbly and outgoing all the time? Or do you want to put her with a dog who is also soft and understanding and is going to let Mary be vulnerable and have someone to depend on? We have matches that go either way. They both work. It just depends on all the other factors at play. But in the end, it's up to the dog. We just read the situation."

As we spoke, others from the p4p contingent trickled into the restaurant—the students and their parents, Miami Phillips and the videographer Jim Gilson. Soon enough, our group had taken over a wing of the restaurant. The back-and-forth chatter was hyper and free-flowing. It reminded me of overadrenalized reporters sitting around the bar late into the evening talking about the firefight or the play-off game or the political debate they had just covered.

For most of the students, it had been their first Bump, and a lot of the conversation centered on the tidal waves of emotion that had swept that prison dining hall. "Bottle that," someone said, "make a fortune." A few people placed friendly wagers about whether, in the end, it would be Sampson or Morgan placed with Josh; the bets were divided about evenly. And Terry made plans with Miami to return to Hazelton in two weeks to instruct the handlers in the specialized training regimens that the Bumped dogs would now undergo. One of the students volunteered her uncle's farm near Wilmington as a site for Madison's "gun work" once she was ready for her Public Access Transfer Training. It had not occurred to me until now that of course a dog that had spent the better part of its life in prison would have to become accustomed to hearing the reports from Tony's hunting rifle.

Kyria and Terry were the first to leave. On her way out, Kyria tapped me on the shoulder, offering a weary smile.

"You once asked me how I don't get burned out doing this," she said. It was as much of a sigh as a sentence. "This is why. Because these are the kind of people we're surrounded by."

Terry put his arm around his daughter and gave her a squeeze. Snow blew through the doorway when they opened it to leave.

"That sponge stuff, dogs sucking up the bad vibes," Miami said when they'd gone. "I think it applies to Terry and Kyria as well."

Chapter Nine

Stone Mountain

B y 5:00 a.m., Claire is settled onto a clean bundle of bedding while her eight newborns squirm at her belly beneath the heat lamps. Her breathing is audible, like a light snore. The humans in the Wilmington headquarters exude about the same vitality; we move as if walking underwater.

The only person with any snap to her step is the indefatigable Renee, who has amassed a three-foot pile of blood-spattered quilts, blankets, and towels beside the front door. As the center's industrial-size washing machine and dryer are still on order, come nine o'clock Renee will load the entire mound into the back of her SUV to take to wash at her apartment.

Meanwhile, April is splayed across the floor of the whelping box whispering in Claire's ear while a few feet away Terry dices cubes of lamb to add to the dog's bowl of milk. Across the room Kyria sits cross-legged on the carpet with her back to the wall, her eyelids fluttering as she scrolls through the e-mails on her cell phone. She has a class to teach later this morning. She vows to make it.

I search out Shaw (who will always be "Blackie" to me) and spot him at the bottom of the dog pile, nearly on his back, suckling like a champ and using his tiny shoulders to nudge away any of his mewling brothers or sisters who have the temerity to intrude on his teat-space. Satisfied that my "godson" can hold his own, I retire to the couch in the front room, where I pretend to fiddle with my notes.

Suddenly there's a commotion in the whelping room. Kyria's voice, then April's. Though they are only a few feet away, for some reason I cannot make out what they are saying. My eyelids fly open and I check my watch. Seven o'clock. I have been dozing for two hours.

I jump up and move toward the voices; all hell is breaking loose in there. Renee and the students are gathering the pups into traveling kennels. Claire is shaking like a paint mixer, her bowl of food untouched. Kyria spreads her hind legs and examines her. She is perplexed. Claire appears to be contracting. But her x-rays distinctly showed only eight tiny shapes in her womb. Kyria dials Terry, who had headed home for a shower and a change of clothes, and then the vet's off-hour emergency number.

Their efficiency overwhelms me. Within five minutes everyone is ready to go, the puppies swathed into their traveling cases and Claire wrapped in a warm beach towel. Kyria is first out the door, carrying Claire beneath a sun-streaked sky so blue that my eyeballs ache. Before trundling her into the back of her SUV, Kyria allows her to stop at a bush. Claire squats to do her business with a pronounced wobble . . . and a ninth puppy pops out!

Kyria and April are stunned. It is a breech birth. The amniotic sac has broken in the birth canal and now dribbles out in tattered sections right there on the lawn. Kyria bends to swoop up the newborn, cuddling it with one arm while stroking Claire with the other. She calls for the scissors and hemostatic clamp. It is a third female. Campbell, they will name her, after the Kentucky army fort, but for now they must cut the umbilical cord and get mother and daughter back inside.

Adrenaline flowing, I head for the yarn I had tucked away in a storage box. I reach it at about the same time I hear Terry's Saturn throwing up gravel as it races into the driveway. I have no new colors, but Kyria suggests tying two lengths around Campbell's scruff, one pink and one white. Renee and the kids have returned with the litter and place seven of the first eight pups back on Claire's teats. Shaw, having been there the longest, is the odd man out to make room for the newest arrival. But Campbell won't suckle. Kyria is preparing a bottle of puppy baby formula as Terry bursts through the door. They decide to put Campbell on an hourly feeding schedule for at least the next twelve hours.

Claire is not looking well. As far as I'm concerned, she deserves her raggedness. Campbell is the twenty-third puppy she has delivered in her young life. Terry is not so assured. He will give her a day to recover but nonetheless telephones the veterinarian and makes arrangements to bring her in first thing the following morning.

In fact, the next day the vet will diagnose Claire with a potentially life-threatening uterus infection. In a way, Campbell's breech birth was a blessing. Had Terry not been so worried that the last, late birth somehow damaged Claire's insides, the infection may not have been discovered until it was too late. But Claire cannot yet have surgery. The puppies need her milk. She is placed on twenty-four-hour surveillance at the vet's office. As it happens, once the puppies have been weaned, Claire will undergo a hysterectomy. She will survive and return to April. She will be barren, but Terry had already determined that this would be her last litter.

Over the next week, for the remainder of my stay, the puppies will thrive, the humans will recover. And we will all look back on this night as a happy and proper christening of the brand-new Wilmington headquarters of paws4people.

But before that, before I head back upstairs that morning to snatch a few hours of sleep, a clearly exhausted Terry stops me and rests a hand on my shoulder.

"Welcome," he says, "to the paws4people family."

The Stone Mountain Inn sits across a lush parkland from the famous mountain itself, a stark and treeless eruption of solid igneous granite towering nearly seventeen hundred feet over the rolling Georgia plain flowering today with new spring growth. The neoclassical hotel's columned front porch offers a direct line of sight to an enormous bas-relief, the largest in the world, carved into the mountain's north face. The sculpture features the three mounted heroes of the Confederacy, Stonewall Jackson, Robert E. Lee, and Jefferson Davis.

After exiting my taxi, I took a moment to study the rock carving before stepping past the rows upon rows of golf bags stacked along the portico. Inside, the lobby swarmed with parents and their children, with veterans and their families, with the usual coterie of paws4people volunteers and trainers and students, with dogs underfoot in every direction. Those who were not participating in tomorrow's annual charity golf tournament, the tradition begun by Jeff Mitchell's father and his boss, had been invited to come anyway and take advantage of Stone Mountain Park's sundry divertissements. There were hiking trails, a children's amusement park, a scenic minirailroad tour, and a cable-car line to the mountaintop. There was even an amphibious "duck" vehicle—half bus, half boat—that traversed the nearby lake.

As I made my way toward the hotel's check-in desk, I spotted among the crowd of golfers several p4p clients whose fame had, as it were, preceded them.

I recognized Melissa Buckles and her four daughters from the many newspaper and magazine stories about them that Terry and Kyria had shared with me. A tall, stately former English teacher, the wife of a marine corps band drum major, Melissa was carrying the infant Aiden in one crooked arm and pushing nine-year-old Erin's manual wheelchair with the other. A few paces behind them, Erin's vested Assistance Dog, Solomon, a big-shouldered chocolate Labrador, sauntered between Melissa's oldest girl, Taylor, eleven, and Erin's identical twin, Jade. Erin and Jade had been born conjoined, and during the surgical procedure to separate them, Erin had suffered a stroke to her spinal cord that left her paralyzed from the chest down.

And out of the corner of my eye, I saw Eliot Swiger leaning over his ten-year-old son Jack's electric wheelchair, adjusting the safety straps and whispering something into the boy's ear. I had watched a video of Jack's Bump with the Golden Retriever Caylie, and everyone who knew Jack warned me that despite his damaged brain, which had been ruptured when he was an infant, he remained a pistol, apt at any moment to take off full speed in his power chair and leave his harried parents in the dust. I imagined that Eliot was imploring his son not to zoom out of his sight through the packed lobby.

Near the front desk, Kyria and CeCe Miller, the former Lakin head inmate trainer now working in Wilmington, were huddled over what looked to be an activities schedule. Just beyond them, at the entrance to the small hotel lounge, Miami Phillips was conversing with Ronnie Sweger, a former US Army Special Forces operator suffering from PTSD. Ronnie had a tight grip on his

Golden Retriever Assistance Dog Trask's leash while keeping one eye peeled on his five-year-old triplets, the tow-headed Brett, Briggs, and Brooks. I had met Ronnie, who is active in veterans PTSD support groups, at several paws4people events. Though he always greeted me cordially, I sensed from his body language that by training and temperament he was leery of reporters. I never pushed it.

I checked in, found my room, threw my bag on the bed, and headed out to the pool area, where buffet tables had been laid out for a cookout later that afternoon. As I scanned the patio, someone grabbed me from behind. When I turned, I was engulfed in a bear hug from a handsome woman with a cascading shock of reddish-brown hair and piercing blue eyes. I recognized her from photos as Carol Mitchell, Jeff's mom, and she welcomed me with a big kiss on my cheek.

"He's still makin' it past the sushi," she said and gave me another tight squeeze. I had spoken to Carol several times by phone, and we had e-mailed back and forth often. But this was our first meeting.

"Record crowd for the tournament this year," she said. "We're overjoyed."

Carol and I settled into filigreed metal chairs around a poolside table, and she told me that her husband, Doug, was out at the golf course seeing to last-minute arrangements. Before I could ask, she hooked a thumb over her shoulder in the direction of the barbecue grill. "Right over there," she said, and sure enough there was Jeff.

He was bent over and stroking a dog whose white coat was flecked with light brown spots. It was Tazie, the Afghan rescue dog. Several children were gathered around them, some in wheelchairs, their own Service Dogs circling the confab. Jeff was engaging the kids in conversation. In his striped Bermuda shorts, checkered polo shirt, and black socks and sneakers, he looked like an overgrown version of one of them. His grin resembled a crescent moon.

I was shocked. I had not seen Jeff since Fort Stewart, when he'd barely been able to look me in the eye. Through the intervening eleven months, Terry had kept me abreast of his progress, particularly since he had switched out his first Service Dog, Caroline, with Tazie. Jeff had improved to the point where he now attended regular group therapy sessions with veterans suffering from similar PTSD symptoms, and he even drove up from Atlanta on occasion to serve as a guest lecturer in Kyria's classroom at the University of North Carolina Wilmington. But nothing had prepared me for the changed person I now saw sitting among those kids. The only vestige of the "old" Jeff that I could discern was his tic of continually pushing his glasses back up the bridge of his nose. Even Tazie appeared so much healthier than the scrawny mutt I remembered from Fort Stewart.

"Life of the party, he is," Carol said with a broad smile.

After a rocky start with Terry, Carol was working closer and closer with p4p now. Terry had named her the organization's veterans' advocate as well as appointed her to the paws4vets admissions board. Admissions board?

"It's a new thing," she said. "I help with the veterans' application screening, but in general I'm kind of like the mom there. If any of our vets are having problems, they call me. If I don't know the answer to the problem, I'll find someone who does. But most of the time I'm just a sympathetic ear."

She shot me a knowing look. "Best job I've ever had."

Despite her current enthusiasm, I knew Carol had been "mighty pissed" when Terry took the Service Dog Caroline away from Jeff some ten months ago. (She'd covered her mouth, reddened, and immediately apologized for "swearing.")

"Letdown isn't a big enough word, not even close to a big enough word," she said. "Terry hurt my child. Jeff did every single thing Terry asked of him. But Terry just never saw that bond between him and Caroline. Doug and I didn't understand that at first. We thought Terry was punishing Jeff for no reason. It was just so frustrating."

She remembered accompanying Terry, Jeff, and Caroline to a furniture store near their home during one of Jeff's Transfer Training sessions. "I'm sitting in the background teary-eyed because I see Jeff doing something he absolutely couldn't do: go out in public. And Terry's just shaking his head and saying, 'This isn't working.'

"So I said, 'What do you mean it's not working? Look at how far he's come.' But Terry never answered me. Just kind of stared at me in that gruff, Terry way. I guess my anger was at the lack of communication. My fear was, you take Caroline away, you've killed my kid. He's not gonna survive. I was very scared. Very scared. In Terry's defense, it took me a while to understand that it's hard to put into words the magical thing that happens between people and their Service Dogs."

This confusion and frustration mounted over the next several weeks, Carol said, until she finally received an e-mail from Terry telling her that he was pulling Caroline. She was in midsentence when I heard a male voice over my shoulder.

"The e-mail basically said that Terry just did not see the love. It was a kiss-off letter."

I turned to face Doug Mitchell. He was a large, broad man, wearing pleated khakis and a blue Windbreaker over his striped yellow polo shirt. A white golf glove protruded from his rear pocket. With his silver mane and weather-beaten face, he may as well have been a walking advertisement for Calloway or Nike.

"I caught the end part of your conversation," he said as he shook my hand and picked up the narrative. "One thing that really got to me—Terry told us that he didn't hear that doggie-baby talk between Jeff and Caroline. This I couldn't understand. A big, tough soldier who's seen things no human being should see in combat is being denied a Service Dog because he doesn't do baby talk? C'mon.

"I was angry," Doug said. "We'd invested a year and a half of our lives in Caroline . . . "

"Not to mention thousands of dollars in travel expenses," said Carol.

Now there was an edge to Doug's voice. "Don't forget, Caroline wasn't living with us full time. Jeff would train with her at Fort Stewart and maybe every once in a while get her for a few days. And I'm thinking, 'No bond?' No bond? How do you expect our son to bond with the dog when he can only keep her two, three days tops?'"

"But things turned out for the best," Carol said.

She placed her hand over her husband's. A whimsical look crossed her face as she described what happened next.

Despite taking Caroline back, Terry nonetheless offered to allow Jeff to keep training with the Fort Stewart group. Whether he would qualify to receive another Service Dog remained unclear. Perhaps he would have to settle for a companion dog, one that had not been trained as thoroughly as a psychological Service Dog to deal with a returning soldier's PTSD. Carol and Doug were skeptical. Once again their son had been made to feel as if he'd failed. Once again he had been made to feel that he was not good enough. But they saw no other options. Jeff's life was at stake, and if a pet dog could help in any way, so be it.

Then only days after the Caroline decision, Terry called Jeff with a request: Could Jeff retrieve Tazie, who had been ejected from the prison program that p4p was overseeing at the medium-security Jesup Federal Correctional Institution near Fort Stewart? Because of her feral upbringing in Afghanistan, Tazie had been unable to adjust to sleeping in her small prison carry-kennel and had displayed such resource-guarding traits as growling and barking when she was led into it at night. Staff Sergeant Ward had picked the dog up and taken her home, Terry told Jeff, but the sergeant could not keep her. Since Terry himself could not make it down to Georgia for a week or so, could Jeff house her until he got there?

As the Mitchells told their story, I sensed Terry's backup plan for Jeff—the one he had hinted at back in the motel outside of Fort Stewart—being put into motion. I wondered if he knew then that Tazie was the key to Jeff's future. Certainly the Mitchells had no idea. They had been genuinely angry at losing Caroline.

Carol picked up the story. "So Jeff comes downstairs and says, 'Mom, I just got a call from Terry. Do you remember that really cool white dog from Afghanistan? She's been kicked out of the Fort Stewart program, and they need somebody to foster her until Terry can figure out what to do with her. Do you want to go down to Fort Stewart with me and pick her up?'

"We jumped in the car the next day," Carol said, and at this I again glanced toward Jeff and Tazie surrounded by the kids. The dog, a mixed-breed Saluki and Anatolian Shepherd as near as anyone could tell, sat placidly by Jeff's side, scooting her rear into his legs.

Tazie captured Jeff's and Carol's hearts from the first moment they met her. She nuzzled Jeff and he kissed her back. She jumped right into Carol's car without a fight. On the drive home from Fort Stewart that afternoon, Tazie laid her head on Jeff's shoulder and kept it there the entire ride. Carol said she nearly swerved and crashed when Jeff, with no prompting, addressed the dog in — yes—baby talk.

The next morning Jeff hooked Tazie on an extra-long leash and left the house to walk her. Carol watched through a window as they ambled down the street together. They were gone but a few minutes when a thunderhead darkened the sky. The wind picked up and the leash began to vibrate. The thunder claps sounded like artillery, and to Jeff's mind the whap-whap-whaps of the vibrating leash were helicopter blades. He dropped facedown on the sidewalk and squeezed his eyes closed. Suburban Atlanta had transformed into Tal Afar.

When he opened his eyes, the first thing he saw was Tazie. She was lying next to him, also splayed across the sidewalk, shivering. He sat up and Tazie stood. He hugged the dog close for a moment, and then they both ran home through the rain.

"Tazie gets it," Carol said. "The same things that trigger something in Jeff trigger something in her. They've both survived the battle zone, and that's part of the trust between them."

The plan was to keep Tazie for ten days until Terry found her another home. That was almost a year ago.

"It didn't take us more than two or three days to see that bond Terry was talking about," Doug said. Then he caught himself, waved his hand.

"No, strike that. To *feel* the bond between Jeff and Tazie that Terry was talking about. There was a change in Jeff, in his heart, I guess is the best way to say it. He was letting the wall down like he never did with Caroline."

"In retrospect," Carol said, "Caroline was an absolute crucial teaching tool to get Jeff ready for Tazie. They may not have been right for each other, but she started to crack open Jeff's protective barrier, and then Tazie just blew it up."

Again I turned, but Jeff and Tazie were gone.

"He went back to the room a minute ago," Carol said. "As far as he's come, he still needs his quiet time alone."

Without thinking, I said, "Maybe it was all God's plan?"

Carol and Doug looked at each other for a long moment. Finally Doug said, "Send a child to war and you get on your knees. That's what happened to us."

Before Jeff shipped off to Iraq, Doug explained, Carol attended Sunday services when she could, but he had lapsed from the Baptist traditions of his childhood. He was, he said, "ashamed and embarrassed" by his lack of spirituality, particularly when his father fell ill with cancer soon after Jeff was deployed.

"We were drowning," Carol said, "only we didn't know it. Then, two weeks after Jeff left, Doug's dad died. As they're rolling Doug's daddy's body out of the house, the mailman comes up the walk and we get our first letter from Jeff. That was not a coincidence. And it didn't stop there."

Not long after, she continued, her mother was diagnosed with terminal heart failure. The family arranged for a Methodist minister—"Pastor Dave," she called him—to visit her mother daily. Every afternoon following Pastor Dave's visit, Carol's mother would ask after Jeff. When was he coming home?

"She was just trying to hold on to see him one more time," Carol said. She lowered her head. "She didn't make it."

These multiple tragedies, she said, combined with the knowledge that their son was in harm's way, hammered home a realization. "It wasn't so much like God was tapping us on the shoulder as much as thumping us over the head.

"So that started our real journey. We not only returned to the Church, but now we're regulars at Disciple classes where you read the Bible cover to cover. Doug and I will take any class Pastor Dave is teaching. And I mentioned coincidences? We do not believe that it was a coincidence that Jeff was home and in the VA Hospital where I just happened to spot that VA newsletter with the story about paws4people."

"It was God's will, I suppose," Doug said.

And perhaps, I thought, also a little bit of Terry Henry's will. Few people, painters mostly, have the ability to see the mind beyond a person's visage. I believe Terry has that gift. And it was at this point that I confessed to Carol and Doug about the conversation I'd had with Terry in the hotel, about Terry telling me he would never give up on Jeff as long as Jeff didn't give up on himself, about Terry winking—winking!—when he spoke to me of forging Jeff's future.

"I've teased him about that, called him an evil genius," said Carol. A broad grin creased her face. "We know now that Terry always kept up hope for Jeff. In truth, I think Terry sees a lot of himself in Jeff. That's why he tried so hard to break down Jeff's barriers . . . "

"And I also think that's why he became more frustrated with Jeff when he couldn't get through to him," Doug said.

Speaking of the evil genius, I asked, where was he? Doug pointed across the pool to a table the farthest away, in the shade of an oak tree. There Terry sat, Chaeney at his feet, deep in conversation with two elegant women I had never seen before.

I wandered over, and he greeted me with a hug before

introducing Elizabeth Dulin and Ali Curtin, two administrators from a nearby private school for autistic children. Paws4people, he said, was arranging for an Assistance Dog to be donated to the school, and in fact there would be a dedication ceremony to that effect tomorrow morning prior to the golf tournament. As they stood to leave, Elizabeth and Ali told me I could meet some of their students then, and off they went. Terry rose, too. He said he was tired and needed a nap.

As we walked together into the hotel lobby, I told him about my conversation with Carol and Doug Mitchell, as well as my shock at Jeff's appearance. Plus, I said, there was now a paws4vets Board of Admissions?

"Things are moving fast with us, and Kyria and I need all the help we can muster," he said. "This private school thing, for instance, is only the beginning. We may have some more coming on board. Kyria and Miami have some other tricks up their sleeves, too. Still, it's good to know the old connections like Jeff are still a part of all of it."

I told him I'd stand him a burger and a soda later at the cookout.

"They're free," he said.

"I know," I said.

It was a gorgeous day for golf. The sun was so bright, the air so crisp, that I almost regretted not taking Miami up on his offer to join his foursome. As I made my way through the parking lot of the Stone Mountain Golf Club, I noticed several limbless golfers—a leg missing here, an arm there—milling among the nearly two-hundred-odd duffers who had entered the tournament.

From the ages and relative fitness of the wounded, I pegged them as either Iraq or Afghanistan veterans. Both of the club's eighteen-hole courses would be full that day, and the fund-raiser's organizers had had to rent extra golf carts to accommodate the overflow.

The clubhouse was jammed with people taking advantage of the breakfast buffet and the open bar—busboys hustled to refill the rapidly emptying jugs of Bloody Mary mix. I found Terry off in a corner of an empty anteroom, by himself naturally, standing guard over a trio of dogs. There was good old Chaeney, but also Jack Swiger's Caylie and Ronnie Sweger's Trask. Across the room, several of Kyria's student-volunteers were herding a pack of their own that I did not recognize. It turned out that Caylie and Trask and the other animals were there to circulate among the golfers throughout the day to remind them what they were playing for. Also on hand was a Golden Retriever named Langley, who was destined for the autistic children's school.

Terry flicked his chin in the direction of the practice putting green, and I spotted Elizabeth, Ali, and what I took to be a few teachers leading a disparate group of kids. When Terry and I reached them, Ali introduced me to the half-dozen students, who ranged in age from six to sixteen. Elizabeth said that their levels of autism ran from slight to profound. Surprising myself, I sat down among them on the grass and started playing silly games—made-you-look, got-your-nose, pulling quarters from their ears.

A few of the children asked me the same questions over and over and over. What's my name? Did I have a dog? Did I want a dog? What's my name? By now I knew enough about the disability to recognize this as a symptom, and when Elizabeth tried to quiet them from "bothering me," I waved her off. I thought of Tracey Gregor, of Ann Bartlinski, of all the p4p family. Of David

Burry: *Patience*. I answered each repetitive question with a smile and a silly face.

Next came an exhibition by a South African Special Forces veteran whose spine had been severed by an Iraqi sniper's bullet. Paralyzed from the waist down, he had started a nonprofit foundation called Stand Up and Play and invented a complex wheelchair—the "Paramobile" he'd dubbed it—that, at the press of a button, raised him to a strapped-in standing position from which he could swing a golf club.

He stood beside a US Army veteran who climbed out of his own wheelchair on one leg to fire golf balls from his modified AR-15 assault rifle. The morning sun was already stifling, and the two, sweating like Semtex, hit and fired a dozen balls at a green several hundred yards across the water. Their accuracy was astounding and drew a loud ovation. Then they announced that they would be stationed on the sixteenth tee to take on all comers in a closest-to-the-pin competition. (Later that night I discovered that they had lost to only two of the fifty or so foursomes who took the challenge.)

Next Kyria, Terry, and Chaeney walked onto the practice putting green followed by a dozen or so p4p clients and volunteers, each accompanied by a leashed dog. They stood on either side of an easel as one of the tournament officials—Doug Mitchell's employer, I guessed—removed a sheet to reveal one of those oversize checks on the wooden stand. It was for $75,000 and was made out to paws4people from the Heroes First Foundation. Someone handed Terry a microphone and he thanked the crowd and made a short speech about how every cent would go toward raising Assistance Dogs.

"I'm not sure if I can articulate how many children and how

many veterans your generosity will save," he said through sniffles.

He swept his arm toward the clients and volunteers. The dogs sat perfectly still. "It is wonderful people like you who give more meaning to the lives of wonderful people like these. And I thank you from the bottom of my heart."

There was the briefest silence—you could have heard a tee drop—before the parking lot erupted in applause. Terry ducked back out of the spotlight and cuddled with Chaeney. As the golf carts fanned out across the course, I jumped on a courtesy vehicle shuttling people back to the hotel. I arrived just in time to see Eliot Swiger rolling his son Jack onto the hoisting platform of a handicapped-enabled bus. They were heading for the interactive children's park. I gave him a hand—his wife, Lisa, was out on the course with Caylie—and once Jack was aboard, Eliot and I took seats across the aisle from him.

The new bus slowly filled—the Buckles family took up the two rows in front of us—and I asked Eliot if he was nervous about keeping track of Jack in a public space without Lisa and Caylie around. He held up a small remote-control device, about the size of a key fob, and flashed a smile that I can only describe as devilish.

"We call this 'the Stopper,'" he said. "I push this button, and it cuts the power to Jack's wheelchair."

At the sight of the Stopper, Jack let out a howl. "I'll be good, Dad. Promise-promise."

Jack and Erin Buckles were joined by two or three other children in wheelchairs and their families, and it took us a bit of time to unload everyone once we reached the park. Despite the Stopper, Jack burst out in the lead with Eliot in hot pursuit; it was almost like a Road Runner cartoon. I let them go and fell in with the Buckles clan and Solomon the chocolate Lab. Melissa's husband, Kevin, was on duty this weekend, so she had packed up their four strikingly pretty daughters and made the trip without him.

Nine-year-old Erin was noticeably smaller than her twin, Jade, but what she lacked in size she made up for in enthusiasm, particularly when we hit the Nerf-ball shooting arena. I had often tried to imagine what must have gone through Kevin's and Melissa's minds when they were told by their pediatrician that Melissa was the one in one hundred thousand pregnant mothers who was carrying conjoined twins, most of whom do not survive. I could not.

Erin and Jade were born attached from chest to navel, with more than half of Erin's heart beating inside Jade's chest. Melissa remembers patting one baby on the back after a feeding and hearing the other burp. Doctors separated the girls when they were four months old—after warning the Buckles that chances were great that at least one, if not both, of their daughters would probably die during the operation. Though Jade came through the procedure comparatively healthy despite the "hole" in her upper torso, Erin was not so lucky. It was only when she Bumped with Solomon several years ago that her life took on a semblance of normality.

"Before Solomon, Erin was so inhibited, like a permanent attachment to my leg," Melissa told me. "In school she would never raise her hand. She was the kid in the wheelchair all the other kids stared at. Now she's the girl with the cool dog. She even joined a power wheelchair soccer league.

"God chooses all our paths," Melissa said. "Some people are called, some people don't listen."

I had been looking all day for Jeff Mitchell. I had not seen him at the golf course; he did not answer his hotel room telephone; and his mother had mentioned that he might join the kids at the park. No go. So I returned to the hotel, where, by early evening, I was sequestered in a corner of the lounge surreptitiously eavesdropping as Ronnie Sweger and a small squad of Wounded Warriors, including the South African Special Operator, traded war stories. There were enough happy golfers filtering into the bar area that I was able to remain inconspicuous. At one point I saw Eliot Swiger slog into the lounge. He looked as if he'd been rode hard and put away wet.

"Long day," he said. "Even with the Stopper."

I bought him a drink and we toasted Jack.

A short while later, I finally spotted Jeff loping through the lobby with Tazie on her leash. I excused myself and caught up with them on a nearby greensward where Tazie was doing her business. For two days, all about us, Assistance Dogs wearing p4p vests had roamed with their "partners" through the hotel's lobby, across its front porch, by the pool patio, and in the surrounding parkland. Not a single hotel worker or "civilian" unaffiliated with paws4people gave them a second look. It struck a memory chord.

"You remember that Georgia restaurant that didn't want to serve us?" I said.

Jeff nodded. "Oh, God, yes. Terry really let them have it."

It had occurred the very day Jeff and I met. Terry and Chaeney and I were in his Saturn, leading a convoy of army vans packed with a dozen soldiers and dogs back to Fort Stewart from a training session at the nearby Jesup Federal Correctional Institution. We'd decided to stop for lunch at a roadhouse nestled along the edge of a spinney of loblolly pines. Terry was more tense than usual.

The previous evening he had ranted about businesses, from airlines to convenience stores, that turned away active-duty service members and veterans accompanied by Assistance Dogs. I had not given the matter much thought. I had read and seen anecdotal stories about a few kooks, but really, what American would try to bar a disabled soldier from walking into a mall or movie theater? I found out that day. The restaurant's hostess immediately freaked at the sight of the squad of uniformed soldiers and their dogs—on leashes—and summoned the manager.

"I'm sorry, sir," he'd told Terry, "but we only allow Seeing Eye Dogs in the restaurant."

"No, I am sorry," Terry said. If his voice were weather, it would have been sleet. "Because under federal law as well as Georgia law, you must accommodate us."

"That's not what I have been told, sir."

"In that case, we either eat here or we call the police, and when they arrive, I will cite the specific federal and state statutes to them."

Terry had whipped out his cell phone and waited. You could almost hear the gears grinding in the manager's head. The other diners looked on and the room fell quiet as a brief game of chicken ensued. Finally a compromise was reached. The manager instructed the hostess to escort our party through a far door and into an empty banquet room. Terry didn't push it. He thanked her and we sat down to our menus.

"Happens all the time," Terry said that day. Then he pulled out what looked like a laminated business card and handed it to me. "I usually carry the federal laws as well as the laws of whatever state I am visiting on one of these."

That last night at Stone Mountain, I could sense that Jeff, too, had been rolling this incident over in his mind since I mentioned it. "Come a long way since," he said. "Still, far to go."

Jeff had been with Caroline that afternoon in Georgia. He told me he still thinks often, and fondly, about his first Service Dog.

"She was pretty soft, and I was wound pretty tight back then," he said. "It was evident kind of immediately that there was something different between the dynamic with Tazie and the dynamic I had with Caroline. Tazie just, well, gets me. And that puts me at ease. Still, I think Caroline's probably in a better place now."

In fact, he said, Caroline was currently working with a physical therapist providing therapy in special ed classes in Charlotte, North Carolina. Jeff told me that he hadn't had a drink in a year, and since pairing with Tazie, he had reduced his daily meds intake from the fourteen antipsychotics and antidepressants he'd been taking when we'd first met to two pills every morning. We talked for a while about the confusing scourge that PTSD has unleashed on our hundreds of thousands of returning veterans. Jeff knew better than most that for all the medical community's breakthroughs, diagnosing the syndrome remains an inexact science, and there exists no biological test that reliably determines who suffers from it.

Still, he added, before the American Psychiatric Association codified the disorder in 1980, the army and VA would most likely have classified him and all the vets like him as paranoid schizophrenics and locked them away who knows where?

"So there's that," he said. He smiled and stroked his dog's ears. "Much rather be here with Tazie than confined to some padded cell."

Jeff Mitchell making a joke about his impairment. Will wonders never cease?

Jeff and I lingered under the stars for a bit longer. He spoke about the anxiety that still overtakes him when he makes appearances at fund-raisers like this, about the veterans groups he meets with and works with, about steeling himself to deliver his lectures to Kyria's students.

"I've gone up and spoken to her students the past two semesters," he said. "Relive my story for them. Basically, I tell them that I'm the kind of nut your dogs will be dealing with."

He pushed his glasses back up the bridge of his nose. "One of the things that Tazie's really helped me with is kind of getting me to take life one moment at a time. I see that's what she's got to do, and I follow her lead. Guys like me, we like to come up with scenarios that are never gonna happen but will stress us out anyway worrying about them.

"Like this golf tournament. I came last year, too, and I spent months beforehand imagining bad things, like I'd have a breakdown in front of everybody, that something would set me off. That never happened. But it didn't stop me from goin' nuts over it. This year, with Tazie, well, things are different. I'm still not great around people, still have a difficult time in, say, enclosed spaces or with sensory-overload-type situations. But I also understand how to focus on the here and now. It's like the AA slogan, you know, one day at a time. For me and Tazie, it's one moment at a time."

Jeff kneeled to refasten Tazie's leash—"She's not good off-leash, got a very, very strong prey drive"—and the two of us strolled back toward the hotel. When I pulled open the front door, he flinched ever so slightly at the loud hum emanating from the bar now overflowing with golfers. It struck me that before acquiring Tazie—or, perhaps, before Tazie acquired Jeff—the noise and crowd might have set him off.

It was then that I mentioned the conversion he'd undergone since that day he'd "barely made it past the sushi."

"It just stuns the hell out of me," I said.

He gave me a sly grin.

"Yeah," he said, looking me straight in the eyes. "I've noticed that being around this organization changes a lot of people."

———————————

I took a step toward the bar, stopped, and walked back outside. My wanderings led me to the edge of the placid Stone Mountain Lake. The duck boats were hauled up on the beach for the night. The moon reflected off the still waters.

Herman Melville once remarked that meditation and water are forever wedded, and I thought of the person I had been when I began this project a year earlier. If not exactly a cynical reporter, then certainly a skeptical one. I recalled myself standing aloof and watching Terry at Fort Stewart berating the poor benighted soldiers, showering them with his version of tough love, and I wondered what I would say to that reporter, to that man, today.

Mostly I guess I'd tell him to look a little deeper, to feel a little deeper. My journey among paws4people had been just that, a reporting trip that had transposed into a personal journey. The mechanisms of traditional journalism—the mechanisms with which I had entered into this project—now fell well short of the kind of stories from the heart that I had witnessed and wanted to tell. Meeting all the kids and veterans and volunteers and trainers and, yes, meeting all those dogs had given me a perspective on life that I think I had previously lacked. It was good.

I was mulling all this when I heard a noise far down the beach. I turned and could make out the silhouette of a person and a dog walking the water's edge. I took a few steps, and in the moonlight and starlight both figures came into relief. It was Terry and Chaeney. I almost called out, but something said no.

Instead I checked the time. It was not too late to call my wife and tell her I love her. That was my first call. I checked my watch again. Soon it would be breakfast time in France, and I knew my son was an early riser.

Postscript

Almost a year to the long night I watched Claire deliver her final litter of puppies, my wife and I attended the 2nd Annual paws4people Family Reunion in North Carolina. We had hoped to bring Liam-Antoine, but he had a bevy of upcoming exams and could not afford to take the time off from school to fly to the States.

The reunion was a three-day weekend affair in Carolina Beach, just southeast of Wilmington, held at one of those retro beachfront hotels reminiscent of 1950s Miami. More than fifty p4p clients attended with their families and dogs. All told, more than 230 members of the p4p "family" descended on the hotel.

I reconnected with old friends like the Mitchells and Sonny and Peggy Morrow, the Buckles and Rachael Wessell, and a large contingent of the northern Virginia volunteers headed by Allison Kaminsky. The veterans Mike Branck and Ronnie Sweger were there —Ronnie had just led an expedition of wounded veterans on an elk hunt out west—as were Terry's parents Jim and Pat. Phil Putney and Lisa Christmas represented the paws4prisons program; the retired Lisa was now living in Florida and, she said, "done with my days behind bars."

Like Carol Mitchell, Lisa Swiger gave both my wife and me a giant hug when she spotted us, and though still confined to his wheelchair, Jack was proud to show me how he had learned to take a few steps with the aid of a cane. Moreover, Jack had submitted a one-minute video to the American Dog Rescue Foundation's You Rescue Me contest—about how Caylie had "rescued" him—and his entry had won the $500 first prize. He was turning it over to p4p. And despite possessing "the Stopper," Eliot and Lisa were still chasing Jack every which way but loose.

April Cook filled me in on the bevy of servicewomen, all victims of military sexual trauma, whom she had convinced to apply for p4p Assistance Dogs. April and Claire had been working a lot outside—in dog parks with her new clients—and she looked fit and tanned. Her smile, her white teeth gleaming against the backdrop of her sun-kissed face, was wider than I'd ever seen it. She informed me that all of Claire's puppies were progressing wonderfully through their prison program training. My "godson" Shaw, she said, was a star pupil. I also made new acquaintances, including the Texas benefactor Arthur Benjamin, who again presented Terry and Kyria with a donation.

The events included a morning of Public Access tests, an Ask a Trainer seminar, and a Pay It Forward roundtable discussion scheduled around social get-togethers such as Friday evening's Wine and Wags on the Boardwalk and Sunday afternoon's Doggie Sand Romp. On Saturday afternoon Terry and Kyria organized a rally competition in one of the hotel ballrooms wherein clients showed off their dogs' skills at obeying commands and pulling wheelchair-bound clients through a makeshift obstacle course.

There was melancholy mixed with the joy. The Bartlinskis could not attend. David Burry, who came with his daughter Ashley, bore the sad news that their youngest, Teresa—tiny "Fang

Fang"—had died some months earlier during her heart transplant surgery. Ed and Ann, he said, were currently in China engaging with government officials and Beijing physicians about opening an orphanage to specifically care for children with heart ailments. And the big US Army Staff Sergeant Paul Tully, whose neck had been broken in Iraq and with whom I'd spent time while visiting Fort Stewart's Wounded Warriors Battalion, had been killed in a motorcycle accident soon after his discharge.

On our first night in town, we walked across the street for dinner at a fish house with Miami Phillips, his wife Shelly, their sixteen-year-old son Ian, and Goose, their black Labrador–Australian Shepherd mix. Shelly was training Goose to become a Service Dog. The fifty-eight-year-old Miami is a fit, angular Georgian with a pecan drawl and a sneaky-sly sense of humor that sands the rougher edges of his strictly business approach to life. He had volunteered his services to paws4people three years ago after a life of sailing the seven seas both in and out of the military service, and he has since become something of the organization's human Swiss Army knife.

Miami had constructed p4p's Web site and database, and with Shelly's input, he also oversees the organization's weekly newsletter. He also has assumed the role of chief fund-raiser, journeying often to Washington to knock on any Congressional door that he suspects might harbor a lawmaker with access to grant money. As the night wore on and we chatted about p4p's future, Miami said that his next project was to raise enough money to open a series of p4p centers around the country that would breed and train Assistance Dogs. Each complex would include not only kennels and training facilities but also veterinary hospitals, special ed classrooms, nursing homes, and hospices.

It is a lofty goal, likely entailing many millions of dollars. But

Kyria, Miami said, had already picked out a name for the complexes: "Riley's Meadows."

"So I'm stuck," he said. "You know Kyria. If she's already got the name, I sure as heck better come up with the money."

I raised an eyebrow. "And Terry?"

"I know, I know," Miami said and chuckled to himself at the ambition. "The one thing about Terry, he'll never, ever get past the *family* aspect of paws4people. It's just not in his DNA. So if I have to help Kyria expand, if I'm here to help make their vision a more corporate reality, my only choice is to make that family bigger. One big, giant family living on Riley's Meadows."

He stared at me with serious eyes. "Why not?"

At this point, with all I'd seen of paws4people, who was I to argue. "Why not?" I agreed.

He was right about Terry, though. Once, during one of our prison rides, I'd asked him what he ultimately wanted out of paws4people.

"I want it to be viewed as the organization that provides the best Service Dogs in the world and helps the most people who want to be helped," he'd said. "Then I'll be able to die knowing that I've put more positive into the universe than negative. And, believe me, I've put a lot of negative into the universe."

I thought of those words the next night, during the buffet dinner in the hotel ballroom that was the weekend's centerpiece. After everyone had dined, Kyria stepped to a podium and welcomed us all. She then proceeded to narrate a slideshow made up of photos of clients and their dogs who had passed their Public Access Transfer Training tests in the last twelve months. Those who were in attendance stood to an ovation when Kyria called their names.

At one point my wife leaned in toward me with an amazed

POSTSCRIPT

look on her face. She had certainly heard enough about the organization from me, but she had never been to a p4p event. She whispered that she could not believe there were forty dogs in the room sitting so quietly under the tables that you would not even know they were there.

Kyria closed out the evening by asking Terry to say a few words. Naturally he waved her off, but after his mother gave him a gentle tug, Kyria and CeCe and Miami and David Burry surrounded him and purposefully formed a sort of moving human wall that edged him from his table toward the microphone stand.

Terry announced that paws4people was close to striking a deal with two more state prisons in West Virginia to provide dog training and that he and Kyria were in the process of organizing several fund-raisers, including a Halloween fun run and, next spring, a Derby4Dogs cocktail party to view the Kentucky Derby. Moreover, he said, as part of the organization's ongoing thrust to raise awareness in the medical community about the horrors of PTSD, p4p had just been chosen by the prestigious Kaiser Permanente Center for Health Research as the sole Service Dog provider to participate in a twelve-month scientific study of the syndrome.

Finally, as he thanked all the volunteers and all the clients and all the trainers and just about everyone associated with the organization for all their hard work, two waiters snuck in behind him carrying what appeared to be an easel draped with a tablecloth. When Terry sensed their presence and spun around, Kyria looked at him with moist eyes, put a finger to her mouth, and took the microphone from his hands.

"Dad, everyone in this room loves you," she said. "Everyone in this room recognizes that there would be no paws4people without you. That you are the heart and soul of this organization. So we all

223

got together, and we'd like you to accept this small token of our gratitude and appreciation."

CeCe pulled the tablecloth. Beneath it, propped on the easel, was a portrait of Terry's first dog, Addie. The portrait was composed of hundreds of miniscule photographs of the faces of the paws4people family.

Terry approached the gift and his knees wobbled. He turned away from the crowd, rested his head against the wall, and wept. My wife gripped my knee so hard I thought she would break it. Everyone in the room stood and clapped. Many cried. Kyria and Jim and Pat moved toward their father and son and embraced him. Terry continued to cry.

Terry Henry cries easily. Oh, as a former navy man, air force counterintelligence operative, and security specialist, he has acted the tough guy on many occasions. But I have also witnessed Terry's tears flow at the memory of the disabled children and traumatized veterans with whom he has placed Assistance Dogs, and his eyes often glisten when he talks about the grace of his daughter, Kyria, or where his own force of fate has led him. I find this admirable.

I do not cry easily. But this night I did.

Acknowledgments

After what you have just finished reading, is it redundant to tell you that, without the cooperation and raw honesty of the members of the paws4people family, *A Dog's Gift* would not exist? Probably. But I'll tell you anyway as my way of extending heartfelt appreciation to each of them for sharing their stories with me while opening up to and putting up with a nosy, prying reporter. Thank you.

I also owe a special thanks to the crack if unofficial editorial committee of Tom Clavin, Bobby Kelly, and David Hughes, whose insights, wisdom, and fine fellowship helped shape this narrative. And as always, I must note my deep appreciation to the indefatigable Nat Sobel and his terrific staff.

Fortune inevitably plays a role in all facets of a book project, and I was fortunate enough to have been guided by two Rodale editors in Alex Postman and the dog-loving Ursula Cary, who not only enhanced the tone and tenor of this book, but also my understanding of human and canine nature. Moreover, if not for the encouragement of Bill Phillips, the editor of *Men's Health* magazine and a dear friend, I would not have begun, much less completed, this project.

Finally, I have been blessed with a family support system that not only endures through thick and thin, but also inspires. For that, I owe a huge debt of gratitude to Denise McDonald and Liam-Antoine DeBusschere Drury.